MEMORY AND REPRESENTATION IN CONTEMPORARY EUROPE

*To my parents,
Martin and Ann Murphy*

Memory and Representation in Contemporary Europe
The Persistence of the Past

SIOBHAN KATTAGO
Tallinn University, Estonia

LONDON AND NEW YORK

First published 2012 by Ashgate Publishing

Published 2016 by Routledge
2 Park Square, Milton Park, Abingdon, Oxon OX14 4RN
711 Third Avenue, New York, NY 10017, USA

First issued in paperback 2017

Routledge is an imprint of the Taylor & Francis Group, an informa business

Copyright © 2012 Siobhan Kattago

Siobhan Kattago has asserted her right under the Copyright, Designs and Patents Act, 1988, to be identified as the author of this work.

All rights reserved. No part of this book may be reprinted or reproduced or utilised in any form or by any electronic, mechanical, or other means, now known or hereafter invented, including photocopying and recording, or in any information storage or retrieval system, without permission in writing from the publishers.

Notice:
Product or corporate names may be trademarks or registered trademarks, and are used only for identification and explanation without intent to infringe.

British Library Cataloguing in Publication Data
Kattago, Siobhan, 1966-
 Memory and representation in contemporary Europe : the
persistence of the past.
 1. Collective memory--Europe. 2. Europe--History--1945-
--Historiography. 3. Memory--Sociological aspects.
 4. Memory--Political aspects. 5. Mental representation--
Europe.
 I. Title
 940.5'5-dc22

Library of Congress Cataloging-in-Publication Data
Kattago, Siobhan, 1966-
 Memory and representation in contemporary Europe : the persistence of the past / by Siobhan Kattago.
    p. cm.
 Includes bibliographical references and index.
 ISBN 978-1-4094-3637-9 (hbk)
 1. Collective memory--Europe. 2. Memorialization--Europe. 3. Representation (Philosophy) I. Title.

D1053.K38 2011
940--dc23
                                                                                              2011027172

ISBN 13: 978-1-138-11102-8 (pbk)
ISBN 13: 978-1-4094-3637-9 (hbk)

Contents

Preface		*vii*
Introduction		1
1	The Slippery Slope of Memory	17
2	Agreeing to Disagree on the Legacies of Recent History	27
3	The Ethics of Seeing: Photographs of Germany at the End of the War	49
4	The Sound of Silence: Reflections on Bernhard Schlink and Gesine Schwan	59
5	Living in the Third Person: The Uncanny Hans Schneider/Schwerte	67
6	Goodbye to Grand Narratives? Moving the Soviet War Memorial in Tallinn	77
7	Memory, Pluralism and the Agony of Politics	97
8	The Fata Morgana of Revolution	109
Postscript: Europe between Past and Future		123
Bibliography		*129*
Index		*139*

Preface

I am grateful for the institutional support of the department of Philosophy at the Estonian Institute of Humanities at Tallinn University and to funding from ETF Grant 8625: 'History as Cultural Memory: Toward an Estonian Mnemohistory.' A sabbatical during the Fall semester 2010 enabled me to concentrate on writing. Students at Tallinn University provided an open forum for the discussion of collective memory in Europe. Likewise, students at the Tallinn University Summer School on 'How Collectivities Remember' in 2007 and the Doctoral School in August 2010 at Åbo Akademi in Vasa, Finland were particularly helpful with discussions about modernity and memory.

'The Slippery Slope of Memory' (Chapter 1) originally appeared in *Alteration of Culture Memory and Local History*, Acta Humanitarica Universitatis Saulensis in Lithuania (2010). 'Agreeing to Disagree' (Chapter 2) was presented at the *European Journal of Social Theory* conference, 'Europe since 1989: Interpreting Social Change' (June 19-21, 2008) at Sussex University. The final, definitive version of this paper was published in the *European Journal of Social Theory*, 12:3, August 2009 by SAGE Publications Ltd. 'The Ethics of Seeing' (Chapter 3) is a much revised book review originally published in *German Politics and Society* (20:3, Fall 2002). The 'Sound of Silence' (Chapter 4) is likewise an extended version of a book review published in *Constellations* (7:4 2000). An earlier version of 'Goodbye to Grand Narratives?' (Chapter 6) was presented at a conference at the Tampere Peace Research Institute, University of Tampere in June 2007. A later version, which has since been revised, appeared in *Constellations* (16:1, 2009) under the title 'War Memorials and the Politics of Memory.' 'Memory, Pluralism and the Agony of Politics' (Chapter 7) was originally published with the *Journal of Baltic Studies* (41:3, 2010) and as a chapter in *Memory and Pluralism in the Baltic States*, edited by Eva Clarita Onken Pettai, (Routledge 2011); both of which are originally available at http://informaworld.com. I am very grateful to the editors of these publications for permission to republish this material here.

For comments on earlier drafts, discussions about the politics of memory in Europe and encouragement to write, my heartfelt thanks to Andrew Arato, Paul Blokker, Karsten Brüggemann, Hubertus Buchstein, Benoît Challand, Jeffrey Goldfarb, Jörg Hackmann, Andrew Hoskins, Tiina Kirss, Marko Lehti, Andres Luure, Peeter Müürsepp, Kristina Norman, Jeffrey K. Olick, Eva-Clarita Onken Pettai, Pille Petersoo, Klemen Slabin, Gesine Schwan, Marek Tamm, Rita Trimoniene, Raivo Vetik, Tõnu Viik, and Vera Zolberg.

My parents and family have supported the idea of a book about European memory, throughout its different, winding phases. I am grateful to the editors at Ashgate Publishing for their help from beginning to end. This book could not have been completed without the close reading, humor and marvelous friendship of Johanna Söderholm.

Siobhan Kattago
Tallinn, 2011

Introduction

What then is time? If no one asks me, I know what it is. If I wish to explain to him who asks, me, I do not know. (St. Augustine)

Hardly a day goes by without some media coverage or commentary about the politicization of the past and the politics of memory. There seems to be no shortage of debates about how to represent the past to ourselves and to the next generation. The recent memory boom is visible in history museum debates, monuments, film and photography, commemorations, political speeches and tourism. Academic studies of memory abound in sociology, philosophy, literature, cultural studies and history. Whether one looks at commemorations of the Second World War, debates over appropriate Holocaust memorials or public apologies for national pasts—the issue of memory seems to have an obsessive hold on the public imagination. Are we experiencing more memory now than before or has the mass media simply made us more aware of the recent past? My sense is that the interest in memory is more than an academic trend or a new way of talking about history. Indeed, the politicization of the past is linked to modern perceptions of time and identity. While our backward glance may be seen as a response to the uncertainties of the future, it has deeper roots in modern conceptions of time. To my mind, there at least three reasons for the centrality of memory in contemporary culture: 1) the modern acceleration of time 2) shift from hard to liquid modernity entailing greater interest in the past and 3) the growing importance of the mass media in everyday life.

The Modern Acceleration of Time

The modern break with tradition, democratization of history, secularization of society and distinction between community and society are among just a few of the phrases associated with modernity. Complementing Pierre Nora's idea of the modern acceleration of history, the German historian, Reinhart Koselleck emphasizes how the break with pre-modernity entails a qualitative shift in our understanding of time (Nora 1996, Koselleck 1985). Beginning with the French Revolution, a different sense of future emerged. While medieval time was predominantly cyclical and contained the Messianic promise of redemption, modern time is open-ended and anticipates an ever accelerating future. The shift to modernity means that 'time is no longer simply the medium in which all histories take place; it gains a historical quality' (Koselleck 1985: 246). Modernity accompanies a shift in our perception of time and historical consciousness. Heralding a kind of new time (*Neuzeit*), modernity brings about a reversal of the structure of time enabling the future to become increasingly more important than the past. Since the Enlightenment and the French Revolution, belief in progress and the infinite perfectibility of science have become modern creeds that we often take for granted.

> Acceleration, initially perceived in terms of an apocalyptic expectation of temporal abbreviation heralding the Last Judgment, transformed itself – also from the mid-eighteenth century – into a concept of historical hope. (Ibid., 36-37)

Koselleck's 'semantics of historical time' is part of his lifelong project, the *Geschichtliche Begriffsgeschichte* (the historical history of concepts) (Brunner ed. 1972-1993). Expressing more than a lexicon of historical concepts, *Begriffsgeschichte* is a method of historical understanding. The purpose of his project is to examine 'the dissolution of the old world and the emergence of the new in terms of the historicoconceptual comprehension of this process' (Koselleck quoted in Tribe 1985: xi). By studying the *Sattelzeit* or dawn of modernity, Koselleck is able to gain insight into modern historical consciousness and temporality. Influenced by Gadamer's philosophical hermeneutics, he examines how historical consciousness is shaped by the cultural and historical traditions that we are born into. For Gadamer, 'history does not belong to us, but we belong to it' (Gadamer 1975: 277). Koselleck interprets Gadamer's retrieval of tradition as a starting point for exposing the contradictions and ruptures within one's own lived tradition. In many ways, Koselleck's work focuses on a central question:

> How, in a given present, are the temporal dimensions of past and future related? This query involves the hypothesis that in differentiating past and future, or (in anthropological terms) experience and expectation, it is possible to grasp something like historical time. (Koselleck 1985: xxiii)

Indeed, Koselleck's distinction between past and future can be linked with Maurice Halbwach's model of frameworks of memory (*les cadres sociaux de la mémoire*) and Nora's places of memory (*lieux de mémoire*). By arguing that the past is a space of experience (*Erfahrungsraum*), Koselleck emphasizes how the past is represented as a kind of topography in maps and timelines. The future, as the horizon of expectation (*Erwartungshorizont*), is qualitatively different from the past because it is open to the unknown and has not yet been experienced. 'The presence of the past is distinct to the presence of the future' (Ibid., 272). The poetic metaphors of the past as a spatial topography are helpful in understanding how experience can be located and concretized into places of memory such as museums and monuments. Likewise, the metaphor of a horizon invokes Gadamer's hermeneutical 'horizon of understanding' and the open horizon of a future full of unknown possibilities.

Since each epoch understands time in a different way—past, present, and future have different meanings at different historical periods. 'Historical time, if the concept has a specific meaning, is bound up with social and political actions, with concretely acting and suffering human beings and their institutions and organizations' (Ibid., xxii). The modern acceleration of time entails more than intensity or speed. As Koselleck notes, it means a completely different sense of temporality in which time is no longer cyclical, but linear and oriented towards the open-ended future. If modernity is associated with belief in a progressively better future, contemporary conceptions of time seem to be marred by the opposite. If anything, one senses more hesitancy towards the future than optimism. Secularization, globalization and a growing mass culture have brought questions of identity to the fore. While we may participate in the same mass culture and consume similar products, the need for a fixed place of identity pushes us further and further towards the past. For it is there, that we seem to find a sense of continuity and stability that is otherwise absent from our everyday life. In many ways, the backward glance of Benjamin's angel of history has become emblematic of the contemporary preoccupation with memory. The angel of history is propelled towards the future while looking back at the ruins of the past.

> Where we perceive a chain of events, he sees one single catastrophe which keeps piling wreckage upon wreckage and hurls it in front of his feet. The angel would like to stay, awaken the dead, and make whole what has been smashed. But a storm is blowing from Paradise: it has got caught in his wings with such violence that the angel can no longer close them. This storm irresistibly propels him into the future to which his back is turned, while the pile of debris before him grows skyward. The storm is what we call progress. (Benjamin 1968: 257-258)

Benjamin's angel of history famously captures how faith in progress and rationality was ruptured by the barbarism of the Second World War, twentieth century ideologies and the Holocaust. Whether examined as the dark side of modernity in Adorno and Horkheimer's *The Dialectic of Enlightenment* or the modern and postmodern debates about the Enlightenment and meta-narratives; the Holocaust and the Gulag challenge a simple reading of modernity as progress. Described as an aporia for historical narration and representation, the Holocaust presents moral and philosophical challenges to modern identity and history (Friedlander 1992). It is at this point that I find the work of Pierre Nora, Zygmunt Bauman and Andreas Huyssen to be helpful. Nora's excavation of the places of French cultural memory links the modern acceleration of history with a growing interest in the past. If change is a permanent feature of modernity, one response to continual change and the uncertainty of the future is the obligation to remember the past. 'The commandment of the hour is thus "Thou shalt remember"' (Nora 1996: 10).

Liquid Modernity and the Shift from Future to Past

Eschewing earlier distinctions between modern and postmodern, Bauman suggests the interesting distinction between hard and liquid modernity. Complementing Koselleck's ideas about the structural change in temporality between pre-modern and modern, he argues that contemporary society is experiencing a second transformation in the structures of both time and space. In various places, most notably *Liquid Modernity*, Bauman argues for qualitative changes from hard modernity rooted in the industrial age of production to a liquid modernity of consumption and uncertainty. Expanding Marx's idea that 'all that is solid melts into air,' Bauman suggests that distinctions between modern and postmodern miss what is qualitatively different in contemporary society. If Marx's idea of the liquidity of modern society was made in the name of new 'new and improved solids' such as communism and the rule of the working class, Bauman suggests that liquid modernity is hesitant about the possibility of any solid future (Bauman 2000: 3).

> The kind of modernity which was the target, but also the cognitive frame, of classical critical theory strikes the analyst in retrospect as quite different from the one which frames the lives of present-day generations. It appears 'heavy' (as against the contemporary 'light' or 'liquefied'); condensed (as against diffuse or 'capillary'); finally, systemic (as distinct from network-like). (Ibid., 25)

If the Fordist factory, bureaucracy and the panopticon represent aspects of hard modernity, liquid modernity is diffused into the globalized shopping mall, internet and advertisement. 'The society which enters the twenty-first century is no less 'modern' than the society which entered the twentieth; the most one can say is that it is modern in a different way' (Ibid., 28). To be modern is to cherish newness and ever-increasing modernization. For Bauman though, liquid modernity is characterized by two features: 'The first is the gradual collapse and swift decline of early modern illusion: of the belief that there is an end to the road along which we proceed, an attainable *telos* of historical change, a state of perfection to be reached tomorrow, next year or next millennium, some sort of good society...' (Ibid., 29) Everything solid melts *without* forming into a new solid. The second feature of liquid modernity is that privatization and individualization accompany the decline of solidity and stability. Large-scale improvements in society are shifted from the state to the individual. '"Fluid" modernity is the epoch of disengagement, elusiveness, facile escape and hopeless chase' (Ibid., 120).

While hard modern temporality is rooted in the French Revolution and the Enlightenment, liquid modern hesitancy toward the future makes the past more attractive. There is a marked shift away from anticipation of the future to memories of the past. Rather than attribute our obsession with the past as a form of pessimism and distrust of the future, Andreas Huyssen argues for a transformation in modern conceptions of temporality akin to Bauman's liquid modernity. 'Thus we are not just experiencing another bout of pessimism and doubt of progress, but we are living through a transformation (*sic*) of this modern structure of temporality itself' (Huyssen 1996: 8). Memories of the past are not captured or relived as 'experience' but rather 're-presentations' of remembered experience. In *Twilight Memories* and *Past Present*, Huyssen articulates the link between memory and representation. 'The past is not simply there in memory, it must be articulated to become memory' (Ibid., 3). If the past is the space of experience, then the process of remembering also involves layers of reconstruction and imagination. Huyssen captures how images of the past in literature, art and museums represent memories of the past as fragmentary traces, shadows and ciphers. 'At the end of the Proustian experience, with that famous Madeline, is the *memory of childhood* (*sic*), not childhood itself' (Ibid.). We cannot retrieve childhood in its entirety, but only a flicker of childhood as it is remembered at a particular time. It is at this juncture of the acceleration of time and the disorientation of identity that memory becomes increasingly linked to that quintessentially modern place of memory and storytelling: the museum.

Memory and the Mass Media

With the omnipresence of the mass media in everyday life, there are more ways to remember and make sense of the past. Representation has shifted not only from an oral to a written culture; but more importantly, from a written to a visual culture. Such a change affects ways in which the past is represented and narrated. Film and photography are powerful media because images simultaneously connect and distance the audience to the past. In their primal sense of immediacy, mass media images link one to the past; however, in their literal suspension of time and narrative, mass-mediated images may also alienate viewers from historical events. Photography and film possess the dual capacity to simultaneously intensify or alienate individuals from a sense of historical consciousness. We are caught in the representation of history 'as if' we, ourselves, were present in this historical event— although curiously outside the event itself. With the development of technology and the mass media, we have the unprecedented ability to archive, catalogue, photograph, film, and record ourselves. As Huyssen notes, the late twentieth century is ironically marked by *both* a culture of amnesia and an obsessive desire to remember. 'The difficulty of the current conjuncture is to think memory and amnesia together rather than simply to oppose them' (Ibid., 7). What does it mean to live in a culture in which the memory of historical events is so ephemeral and, yet at the same time, obsessed with chronicling and storing every human activity? Historical events are, on the one hand, recorded with minute attention to detail. Yet, on the other hand recent events are quickly forgotten as a new 'story' replaces the old. It was Adorno who first captured the museal-like quality of modern representation.

> The German word, "museal" (museum-like), has unpleasant overtones. It describes objects to which the observer no longer has a vital relationship and

which are in the process of dying. They owe their preservation more to historical respect than to the needs of the present. (Adorno 1967: 175)

Adorno's concept of museal has an uncanny quality to it because the function of a museum becomes more like a mausoleum than archive. 'Museum and mausoleum are connected by more than phonetic association. Museums are like the family sepulchers of works of art' (Ibid., 175). Hermann Lübbe later adds to Adorno's musealization by moving the concept from the formal museum to that of everyday life (Lübbe 1983). Not only is time accelerating; but technological change entails a contraction and shrinking of the present. 'In short, the contraction of the present entails a process whereby the space of time for which we can calculate our living conditions with a degree of constancy is shortened' (Lübbe 2009: 159). What distinguishes contemporary society from previous ones is the knowledge that most of the things surrounding us will soon be obsolete. This conscious knowledge of obsolescence means that the present shrinks in duration when compared with the perception of the present in previous periods of history. As a result of this contracting present, individuals have a greater need to catalogue, record, archive and store things before they are soon replaced by something else. 'Let me reiterate my view that the contraction of the present as outlined here, which complements the process of cultural museumification, represents a necessary but by no means sufficient condition for museumification' (Ibid., 162). Echoing Nietzsche, Lübbe diagnoses contemporary society as obsessed with representations of the past. Reflecting on Lübbe's broader reading of musealization, Huyssen writes that,

> Lübbe showed how musealization was no longer bound to the institution of the museum, understood in the narrow sense, but had come to infiltrate all areas of everyday life. Lübbe's diagnosis posited an expansive historicism of our contemporary culture, and he claimed that never before had a cultural present been obsessed with the past to a similar extent. (Huyssen 1996: 22)

The phenomenon of musealization is visible in commemorations, film, photography, Internet archives and television. The more uncertain the future appears, the greater the desire to find solace and security in the past. The musealization of the past is connected with changing perceptions of time and space—as time accelerates and the present shrinks, the past seems to be captured, reconstructed, copy/pasted, blogged, tweeted and frozen at a dizzying pace. Like Huyssen and Lübbe, Baudrillard recognizes the musealization of everyday life. 'The museum is now everywhere, like a dimension of life itself' (Baudrillard 1983: 15). The mass media age has not only altered our understanding and remembrance of recent history, but has also changed the ways in which we identify and situate ourselves within the flow of historical events. By supplying a steady stream of stock images ranging from documentary footage to television dramas and cinema, an iconic vocabulary of images has developed. Cultural memory, as the indirect remembrance of the past that is linked to the present is both intensified and lessened through the image database of the mass media. Koselleck's description of modernity as future-oriented and Bauman's conception of liquid modernity helps us to situate stories of the past within the framework of liquidity, fragility and uncertainty. Likewise, the shift away from the future towards the security of the past is accompanied by an increasing musealization of everyday life as the mass media offers more possibilities for representing the past.

Cultural Memory in the Information Age

With the advent of the Internet, we've come to expect easy digital access to the past. With a click of the mouse and the right hotlinks, history seems to literally unfold before our very eyes. Yet, there is something deeply troubling about our near obsession with storing the past. Are we really more in touch with the past than before or has the digital age ushered in a false smugness? Nietzsche's ascerbic critique of 19th century historicism still offers insight into our 21st century 'historical fever' (Nietzsche 1980: 10). By trying to capture every aspect and detail of the past, we risk losing sight of the present. History has to be useful *for life*; it shouldn't take us away from it. Nietzsche argues for the necessity of finding a balance or horizon between memory and forgetting. To put it simply, he cautions against the tendency to become a 'gravedigger of the present.' In his mind, there are three different kinds of historians or gravediggers: monumental, antiquarian and critical. Monumental history is reductive and simplifies the ambiguous complexity of historical choices. Large events and heroes are contrasted with the ordinariness of contemporary life. Events in the past form a great chain or grand narrative—culminating in the paucity of the present. Nietzsche cautions against a monumental vision of the past because it tends to dwarf the present by calling undue attention to heroic ruptures and breaks within ordinary time.

> Thus, whenever the monumental vision of the past rules over the other ways of looking at the past, I mean the antiquarian and the critical, the past itself suffers damage: very great portions of the past are forgotten and despised, and flow away like a grey uninterrupted flood, and only single embellished facts stand out as islands... (Ibid., 17)

Antiquarian history, on the other hand offers a pious vision of the past. Like the antique collector, the past is preserved uncritically for the sake of preservation. As such, the past becomes a place of consolation and reassurance. When the antiquarian vision of history dominates, Nietzsche detects the 'odour of decay' (Ibid., 21). With the emphasis on preservation for the sake of preservation, the present loses its link to the antiquarian past.

> When history serves past life so as to undermine further and especially higher life, when the historical sense no longer preserves life but mummifies it: the tree dies naturally, beginning at the top and slowly dying towards the roots – and in the end the root itself generally decays. (Ibid.)

The present is eclipsed by an uncritical appreciation of the past. Finally, the critical historian condemns and judges the past based on the needs of the present. While a critical sense of history is necessary so that individuals in the present can judge the past rather than revere or preserve it, Nietzsche criticizes excessive critique because it too easily leads to a denial of the link between past and present.

> It is always a dangerous process, namely dangerous for life itself: and men or ages which serve life in this manner of judging and annihilating a past are always dangerous and endangered men and ages. For since we happen to be the results of earlier generations we are also the results of their aberrations, passions and errors, even crimes; it is not possible quite to free oneself from this chain. (Ibid., 22)

Nietzsche's observations on the abuse of a historical sense, whether monumental, antiquarian or critical still ring true today. Great leaders and epochs loom large as cultural 'islands' of the past while our mass culture thrives on antiquarian oddities and quaint theme parks. The building of memorials and museums coupled with the re-naming and demolition of older ones is a perennial point of contention. In this age of information overload, where yesterday's newspaper is already an antique, the present is often reduced to a minute nanosecond. Obsessed, as we are, with archiving our personal pasts—in family albums, genealogies, videos and digital cameras—all experience is increasingly digitally mediated. Ours seems to be an age of instant memorialization. It is difficult to simply experience an event without recording or capturing it for later viewing. Caught on vacation without a camera, we somehow feel that we are missing something without the mediation of its visual representation. Whether or not we actually look back at the photos that we took is of lesser importance than the actual snapshots that magically validate our experience as authentic and meaningful. The camera placates our fears of forgetfulness by capturing the moment. Our obsession with memory is driven by an injunction against forgetting. The present exists for us as a kind of 'memorial culture.' Because we are saturated with images of the past through de-contextualized documentary film footage, cd-roms, websites, audio recordings, history books, novels, museum exhibitions, and memorials, the past becomes a virtual treasure chest to be ransacked at will. By blurring the line between information and entertainment, the mass media provide the illusion of re-experiencing the past. With this curious distortion of past and present, we experience time differently. It is dilated and seems to exist simultaneously within the present.

But do the mass media help us to remember more? With the speed of contemporary technological change, old media become obsolete faster than we can translate the data into a new readable form. Paper once filled the national archives, now they include celluloid, outdated hard drives and unreadable databases. So what happened? And how might the information age affect our cultural memory? In many ways, Siegfried Kracauer's astute observation that the things of everyday life are more revealing than philosophical systems may illuminate our peculiar predicament.

> The position that an epoch occupies in the historical process can be determined more strikingly from an analysis of its inconspicuous surface-level expressions than from that epoch's judgments about itself. Since these judgments are expressions of the tendencies of a particular era, they do not offer conclusive testimony about its overall constitution. The surface-level expressions, however, by virtue of their unconscious nature, provide unmediated access to the fundamental substance of the state of things. (Kracauer 1995: 75)

Our historical fever and obsession with the past are immediately visible in the multitude of digital collections and archives. Kracauer's emphasis on the mundane and quotidian provides a fresh approach to understanding how new information technologies are affecting our sense of time and history. Places where information is stored such as collections, archives and digital archives provide 'unmediated access' to our perception of the past.

Collecting and Archiving

Any set of things no matter how small can be a collection. From stamps to rare books and paintings, a narrative is given to organize the objects. The collector is not interested in the function of the objects, but in the stories that these objects house. As Walter Benjamin wryly noted, 'The period, the region, the craftsmanship, the former ownership—for a true collector the whole background of an item adds up to a magic encyclopedia whose quintessence is the fate of his object' (Benjamin 1968: 60). Objects become souvenirs (or places of memory) inspiring recollection. They are ruins or traces of a bygone time. As owners of collections, we are heirs to a past and progenitors to a possible future. This passion for collection has taken on a new twist with eBay, blogs, Facebook and YouTube. Concurrent with the speed of technological change is our desire to stand still and find a link—no matter how tenuous—to a warmer past. Collections store memories and fixate identities. Here again, Benjamin rings true: 'every passion borders on the chaotic, but the collector's passion borders on the chaos of memories' (Ibid.). The collector has his or her own sense of order that he bequeaths to his things. Without such a narrative, the found objects are no longer collectibles worthy of another's gaze, but oddities destined for forgetfulness. When something enters a collection, it has secured a foothold in our memory. When Otto Bettmann fled Germany in the 1930s, he left with a trunk full of otherwise random pictures that later became the powerful Corbis collection. Many documentary stock images owe their sustenance to his chaotic passion for collecting the flickering images of recent history. Whether images, books, or china; collections are reduced to things that somehow evoke a glimpse of the past. They are 'things' that someone, like Bettmann, deemed worth salvaging from the dustbin of history. Whether they finally end up on someone's shelf, a second-hand store or in a museum as part of a blockbuster exhibition, the objects are still things suffused with whimsical meaning.

Collections can be private, but archives are by nature meant for public display. Originating from the Greek *arkheia* or town hall, the archive is, by definition, 'a repository for memories or information: *the archive of the mind*' (*American Heritage Dictionary*). Historically though the conception of the archive has already gone through a dramatic sea change even before the appearance of the Internet. In pre-capitalist societies, memory was in the hands of the church, state, and noble families. Archives were maintained and used by scholars and priests rather than by society in general. In many ways, Pierre Nora's ruminations on memory illuminate our present situation. 'Modern memory is first of all archival. It relies entirely on the specificity of the trace, the materiality of the vestige, the concreteness of the recording, the visibility of the image' (Nora 1996: 8). In the general introduction to his edited volumes on French national memory, Nora reflects on the structural shift that the category of memory is undergoing in a mass media age. 'We suffer from a hypertrophy of memory, which is inextricably intertwined with our sense of memory's loss and concomitant institutionalization' (Ibid., 9). The obsession with storing the past accompanies a deep awareness of the loss of traditional life. Because the pace of everyday life is so fast, we try to grasp whatever remains and fragments we can. The past validates our fragile foothold on the present. 'What we call memory is in fact a gigantic and breathtaking effort to store the material vestiges of what we cannot possibly remember, thereby amassing an unfathomable collection of things that we might someday need to recall' (Ibid., 8). Collections, card catalogues and archives bequeath an order to the mountains of information and detritus surrounding us.

While traditional collections and archives house original objects; the Internet and visual media store copies and simulations. Photography was the first stage in the blurring of original and copy. Likewise, Andy Warhol's prints proved the futility of trying to distinguish between the two. With the Internet, the line between referent and copy is completely distorted because 'there is no there, there.' The Internet heralds a structural transformation not only of our systems of information storage and retrieval but more importantly of how we think about ourselves as historical beings. What and how we remember are irreparably altered. As James Gleick says,

> Meanwhile, in its unofficial way, the Internet is transforming the way information is stored. The traditional function of libraries, gathering books for permanent

storage or one-at-a-time lending, has been thoroughly confused. Archiving of the on-line world is not centralized. *The network distributes memory* (*sic*) (Gleick 1999).

Internet experts such as Stewart Brand caution that we are becoming cultural amnesiacs (Brand 1999). The rapid obsolescence of media technology blocks our access to the past because we will not be able to read the old files. Our fantastic short-term memory comes at a very heavy price because in the long run, we forget more. Whereas paper can be read by anyone, files stored in outdated computer languages are easily lost in space. Arguing for the necessity of a long-term time frame, Brand and his colleagues are in no way harkening back to a pre-computer age. Rather they are quick to point out the irony of our information age. We seem to have more information than before, but the speed of technological change obfuscates our ability to 'read' the texts. While the past seems infinitely accessible, computers cannot create a living link between past and future. Acutely aware of the power of the Internet, Brand cautions against the Faustian seduction of technology and argues for a responsible use of digital media. He doesn't advocate a return to the old Smith-Corona but attentiveness to how the Internet is altering our sense of time and historical consciousness. The Internet indulges the antiquarian in us by literally preserving infinite amounts of information. Virtual archives have merged with musty attics. As Gleick bleakly observes,

> The Internet turns a large fraction of humanity into a sort of giant organism – an intermittently connected information-gathering creature – and really, amnesia doesn't seem to be its fatal flaw. This new being just can't throw anything away. It is obsessive. It has forgotten that some baggage is better left behind. *Homo sapiens* has become a packrat. (Gleick 1999)

So we are back to Nietzsche and the 19th century. We have to find a balance between the historical and unhistorical. Not everything is memorable. The human ability to adapt and place events into perspective is central for keeping a perspective on life. Whether Nietzsche's antidotes of the unhistorical (forgetfulness) or the ahistorical (art and science) are sufficient is an open question. Nonetheless, there is a correlation between the speed of everyday life, fragmentation of individual identity and obsession with the past. Nietzsche's sharp condemnation of the 19th century sentiment as 'gravediggers of the present' is deeply unsettling and perhaps also unfair—but that does not mean that it is not worth thinking about. On the contrary, the digital media age seems to encourage more storage and categorization of things from the past. It is Nietzsche's central theme, namely that the past does and should matter, *within* the light of the present that is important to keep in perspective.

* * *

Although each generation discovers new ways to order the chaos around them, the desire to remember and tell stories about the past is as old as the goddess of memory herself. In the Greek world, memory was personified in the titan goddess, Mnemosyne. As the daughter of time (Kronos) and earth (Gaia), Mnemosyne had the gift of reason and the ability to name all objects that we now remember. As a mythological figure, Mnemosyne personifies the mysterious combination of memory, imagination and storytelling. According to Hesiod, Mnemosyne slept with Zeus for nine consecutive nights and gave birth to the nine muses: Clio, the muse of history, Urania, of astronomy, Melpomene, of tragedy, Thalia, of comedy, Terpsichore, of dance, Calliope, of epic poetry, Erato, of love poetry, Polyhymnia, of songs to the gods, and Euterpe, muse of lyric poetry. If the muses each inspire particular manifestations of creativity, Mnemosyne is the mother of all creativity. Embodying memory, she is able to order the flow of time into a narrative form that can be remembered. Combining experience and imagination, memory is an integral part of the human condition—whether in its ancient Greek or modern manifestations. Mnemosyne is thus by implication not only the goddess of memory but the mother of storytelling. Narrative and representation are attempts to cast chaos into order, to make sense of things that would otherwise seem random, chaotic and meaningless. Whether manifest as myth, history, tragedy, philosophy, song or dance—all recorded human activity has its origin in Mnemosyne, the goddess of memory.

The various chapters in *Memory and Representation in Contemporary Europe: The Persistence of the Past* are reflections on different aspects of memory in contemporary Europe. Why do certain places and not others symbolically capture the past and freeze time? Likewise, why does the process of memory, as a fluid and changing activity, seem to prevent its own solidification? The chapters reflect not only on the persistence of the past as a theme linked to media, modernity and time, but also discuss the politics of memory within a changing Europe. The first two chapters were written on the occasion of the twentieth anniversary of the fall of communism. 'The Slippery Slope of Memory' (Chapter 1) analyzes different ways of coming to terms with a difficult past. Discussing Timothy Garton Ash's prescient outline of the problem of how to deal with the past, the essay argues for the fluidity of past and present as well as on the duel dangers of the sacralization and trivialization of memory. 'Agreeing to Disagree' (Chapter 2) addresses the question of whether Europe even needs a common memory of World War II and the post-war period. In this longer essay, the legacy of the past as both an inheritance and a burden is addressed. Framed within the context of a traumatic understanding of the past, 'Agreeing to Disagree' suggests that there are three broad narratives about World War II: a West European, East European/former Communist and Russian/Soviet. Each of these narratives locates the memory of the Holocaust in a different way. In reflecting on this matrix, I maintain *both* the centrality of the Holocaust and the importance of plurality.

The next three chapters analyze cultural examples from Germany after unification. These chapters focus on uncanny places of German memory as represented in novels, photographs and individual biographies. 'The Ethics of Seeing' (Chapter 3) discusses the ideological power of documentary photographs taken in Germany at the end of the war. Reflecting on Dagmar Barnouw's *Germany 1945* and Barbie Zelizer's *Remembering to Forget*, the essay is also a meditation on Susan Sontag's concern with the power of documentary photography to shape memories of the past. 'The Sound of Silence' (Chapter 4) compares Bernhard Schlink's novel *The Reader* with Gesine Schwan's book, *Politics and Guilt*. Here, I examine the power of silence—from repression and evasion to how silence affects the next generation. In looking back one might say that both Schlink and Schwan suggest that one has a moral responsibility to address the past, *whether* one wants to or not. Connected to 'The Ethics of Seeing' and 'The Sound of Silence', the essay 'Living in the Third Person' (Chapter 5) reflects on the life of one individual who tried to live by the motto that not only is the past a foreign country, but also a different person. 'Living in the Third Person' examines how a former SS officer, Hans Schneider officially 'died,' renamed himself Hans Schwerte, remarried his wife and adopted his child only to later become a well-respected professor of German literature in West Germany. The life of Schneider/Schwerte is an uncanny example of self-transformation from authoritarianism to democracy.

The next two chapters, 'Goodbye to Grand Narratives?' (Chapter 6) and 'Memory, Pluralism and the Agony of Politics' (Chapter 7) deal with examples from the Estonian political landscape. 'Goodbye to Grand Narratives?' suggests that the controversy accompanying the re-location of a Soviet-era war memorial was testimony to what Tony Judt called the 'unraveling' of post-war memories. The comfortable cold war narratives of winner and loser, liberator and fascist literally crumbled at the feet of a solitary sculpture in the center of the Estonian capital. 'Memory, Pluralism and the Agony of Politics' discusses the dangers of reading the past through the eyes of victimhood. Taking issue with Schmitt and Mouffe's antagonistic politics based on the dichotomy of friend and foe, I suggest a greater appreciation of pluralism in the sense of Arendt and Berlin. In many ways, the essay is linked with earlier themes and argues for a richer understanding of pluralism over a dogmatic and antagonistic representation of the past. 'Memory, Pluralism and the Agony of Politics' likewise attempts to steer through the difficulties of relativism and the temptation to use the past as a weapon against political opponents. The final chapter, 'The Fata Morgana of Revolution' (Chapter 8) highlights how memories of revolutions are part of the story of modernity. 1989 has joined the pantheon of earlier revolutions. Symbolizing radical newness and rupture, revolutions are the pinnacle of political action. Reflecting on Arendt's ideas about revolution, the essay analyzes their ephemeral and transitory nature. The postscript discusses the legacy of totalitarianism and the revolutions of 1989. The issue is less of whether one should remember, but rather *how* to internalize the various lessons of the past for the future of Europe.

One could say that the challenge of a book about memory lies in its seeming randomness and incoherence. That is, to some extent true. Reflections on memory are not always read from front to back—but rather offer the reader the chance to read the parts that are of interest to them at a particular moment. Likewise, chapters do not provide a neat argument with conclusive findings. But, the more that I teach, write and think about memory, the more I become convinced of its fragmentary and ephemeral nature. The chapters in *Memory and Representation in Contemporary Europe: The Persistence of the Past* thus offer the reader occasions upon which to take stock of different but overlapping contours of past and present in contemporary Europe. Looking back, they are united in their intellectual reference points and influences. In addition to the seminal work of Nietzsche, Gadamer, Halbwachs and Nora, there are four thinkers whose work permeates all of the chapters, that of Arendt, Berlin, Judt and Sontag. The book thus stands literally on the shoulders of giants. Why have I singled out these thinkers and not others? Simply because these are the thinkers, to whom I have returned to, over and over again as a reader, teacher and writer. Although they are different, they share deep moral convictions and poetic styles of writing. Moreover, they are masters of the essay as a literary form of writing.

Arendt is certainly a strong voice haunting this book. From her controversial ruminations on the banality of evil to her majestic plea for new beginnings and the need to think from the point of view of the other person, Arendt is a rich source of inspiration. Her discussion of pluralism complements that of Isaiah Berlin. Both recognize the allure and dangers of trying to fit the complexity of the world into one philosophical or ideological system. Berlin's arguments against monism and passionate plea for pluralism are an integral theme throughout this book. What links Arendt and Berlin to Sontag's work is a deep appreciation of literature. Whether found in Kafka, Broch or Benjamin, the poetic imagination is acknowledged as an important expression of the link between past, present and future. Sontag's influence is most visible in her prescient reflections on photography. To my mind, she is unparalleled in her assessment of the power of the image to enforce and re-enforce a moral position. The final giant whose influence is felt in almost every chapter is that of Tony Judt. Unique in his combination of historian, moralist and public intellectual, this book would be unimaginable without his polemic observations on post-war Europe. By adding the suffix *mis* to memory, Judt added another dimension to the dichotomy between memory and forgetting. A mis-memory does indeed contain a grain of truth, but is somehow off the mark and remembered as the entire truth. Likewise, the metaphor of the unraveling of memory invokes Penelope as she spins her cloth each day only to unravel it in the evening. Memory of the past defies completion—parts are woven together, while other pieces unravel. What links all four writers together is a common concern with the old problem of evil. Defiant against cynicism and relativism, there is a burning sense to try and understand the moral choices that individuals make within the context of their times and to acknowledge the legacy that is the direct or indirect consequence of those actions.

Memory is a *re*-presentation of past experience. One can neither recall everything nor re-live something that happened in the past. Memory, by its very nature is fragmentary, episodic, unpredictable, and yet full of meaning for the one who remembers. One could say that it is the very impermanence of memory that seems to defy representation. Whether expressed in historical documents, novels, monuments, poetry or film—there is an explicit attempt to catch meaningful traces of the past for future generations. The act of memory recalls and interprets the past in both its positive and negative aspects—as tradition and traumatic burden. Regardless of whether memories of the past are written, sculpted or captured on film—as representations, they have a way of taking on a life of their own.

References

Adorno, T. 1967. Valéry Proust Museum, in *Prisms*, trans. Samuel and Shierry Webber. Cambridge, MA: MIT Press.
Assmann, J. 1995. Collective Memory and Cultural Identity, trans. John Czaplicka. *New German Critique*, no. 65, Spring/Summer, 125-134.
Baudrillard, J. 1983. *Simulations*, trans. Paul Foss, Paul Patton and Philip-Beitchman. New York: Semiotext(e).
Bauman, Z. 2000. *Liquid Modernity*. Cambridge, MA: Polity Press.
Benjamin, W. 1968. Theses on the Philosophy of History, in *Illuminations*, trans. Harry Zohn. New York: Schocken Books.
Benjamin, W. 1968. Unpacking my Library: A Talk about Book Collecting, in *Illuminations*. New York: Schocken Books.
Brunner, O. ed. 1972-1993. *Geschichtliche Grundbegriffe: Historisches Lexikon zur politisch-sozialen Sprache in Deutschland*, 8 vols. Stuttgart.
Friedlander, S. ed. 1992. *Probing the Limits of Representation: Nazism and the "Final Solution"*. Cambridge, MA: Harvard University Press.
Gadamer, H.G. 1975. *Truth and Method*, trans. Joel Winsheimer and Donald G. Marshall. New York: Crosswood Publishing.
Gibson, W. 1999. 'My Obsession'. *Wired*, April 7. Available at www.wired.com/wired/archive/7.01<7ebay.html. Accessed April 8, 2010.
Gleick, J. 1998. Fast Forward, the Digital Attic: An Archive of Everything. *The New York Times*, April 12. Available at http://www.nytimes.com/1998/04/12/magazine/fast-forward-the-digital-attic-an-archive-of-everything.html?n=Top/Reference/Times%20Topics/People/G/Gleick,%20James&pagewanted=all. Accessed April 8, 2010.
Gleick, J. 1999. *Faster: The Acceleration of Just about Everything*. New York: Pantheon Books.
Halbwachs, M. 1992 (1941). *On Collective Memory*, trans. Lewis Coser. Chicago, IL: University of Chicago.
Huyssen, A. 1995. *Twilight Memories: Marking Time in a Culture of Amnesia*. New York: Routledge Publishing.
Huyssen, A. 2003. *Present Pasts: Urban Palimpsests and the Politics of Memory*. Palo Alto, CA: Stanford University Press.
Koselleck, R. 1985. *Futures Past: On the Semantics of Historical Time*, trans. Keith Tribe. Cambridge, MA: MIT Press.
Kracauer, S. 1995. The Mass Ornament, in *The Mass Ornament: Weimar Essays*, trans. Thomas Y. Levin. Cambridge, MA: Harvard University Press.

Lübbe, H. 1983. *Zeit-Verhältnisse: Zur Kulturphilosophie des Fortschritts*. Graz/Vienna/Cologne: Verlag Styria.

Lübbe, H. 1992. *Im Zug der Zeit: Verkürzter Aufenthalt in der Gegenwart*. Berlin: Springer Verlag.

Lübbe, H. 2009. The Contraction of the Present, in *High-Speed Society: Social Acceleration, Power and Modernity*, edited by Hartmut Rosa and William E. Scheuerman. University Park, PA: Pennsylvania State Press, 159-178.

Nietzsche, F. 1980 (1874). *On the Advantage and Disadvantage of History for Life*, trans. Peter Preuss. Indianapolis, IN: Hackett Publishing.

Nora, P. ed. 1996. General Introduction: Between Memory and History, in *Realms of Memory: The Construction of the French Past*. New York: Columbia University Press.

Nora, P. 2002. Reasons for the Current Upsurge in Memory. *Eurozine*. Available at http://www.eurozine.com/articles/2002-04-19-nora-en.html. Accessed March 13, 2007.

Tribe, K. 1985. Translator's Introduction, in *Futures Past: On the Semantics of Historical Time*, trans. Reinhart Koselleck and Keith Tribe. Cambridge, MA: MIT Press.

Chapter 1
The Slippery Slope of Memory

Anniversaries provide the occasion to look back and reassess the past from the perspective of the present. One doesn't just look back from any place or time, but from a particular location and particular time in the present. Our point of recollection, remembrance, and reassessment is 'the now'—however fleeting or fixed we may perceive that moment to be. With the mass demonstrations of ordinary East European citizens for freedom in 1989, the fall of communism has brought about a more open society in each of the former communist countries with the exception of Belarus. Each former communist country has its own national story of suffering and liberation within the larger tapestry of that 'place' called East and Central Europe, the Soviet bloc or former Soviet Union. Twenty years on, prepositions of *pre* and *post* are still used: pre-war, post-war, post-communist, post-Soviet. Each preposition qualifies and emphasizes the transitional aspect of time. Pre and post link the noun to a bounded period of time: World War II and communism.

1989 is seen as an *annus mirabilis* or year of wonders, representing the dramatic break from communism, state-planned economies as well as re-entry into Europe. Twenty years on, freedom seems to have lost some of its magnetic and miraculous attraction. Amidst relatively low voter turnout, economic downturn and disappointment with the difficulties in adapting to new economic and social conditions, anniversaries and commemorations provide an occasion to rethink some of the reasons for democratic change. In any transition, advisors come and go, but the major cast of characters stays largely the same. The drama of revolutionary politics cannot compare with the mundane reality of everyday party politics. Since there is not a director with a God's eye view who can call for new actors, a certain process of selection has to take place within the national cast of characters. In the last 20 years, both the communist and Nazi pasts have been opened up for historical examination and a renewed discussion of totalitarianism has emerged. Although modern technology provides individuals with unprecedented means to capture and freeze moments of the past, *how* experiences of war and communism are interpreted and woven into meaningful narratives is far from neutral. The dangers of opening up Pandora's box occurs when individuals fall inside and remain fixated in the past, seeking revenge rather than reconciliation and justice. Particularly because memories of the past invoke truth and facticity, the stage is set for clashing interpretations. All too often, national stories fall into the narrative of winners and losers, liberators and occupiers, friend and foe.

Too much memory makes one a slave to the past, while forgetfulness denies history and one's own link to the past. As Nietzsche cautioned in the 19th century, a balance between the historical and unhistorical is required for the health of individuals, cultures and nations. Criticizing the tendency to diminish the present in the shadow of the past, Nietzsche characterizes the feverish quality of a hyper historical sense. 'There is a degree of insomnia, of rumination, of historical sense which injures every living thing and finally destroys it, be it a man, a people or a culture' (Nietzsche 1980: 10). Granted that Nietzsche's reflections are general and not intended for contemporary discussions of democracy and memory—his metaphor of a balance between memory and forgetting is more relevant that ever.

Coming to Terms with the Past: Whether, When, Who and How

Questions about how to come to terms with a difficult past have been associated with many goals: truth, justice and recognition of guilt as well as consolidation of democracy, national healing, cleansing and reconciliation. Timothy Garton Ash raises the important question of whether there indeed exists a clear correlation between how a nation comes to terms with its past and the consolidation of a democratic culture. Since World War II, West German discussions of how to come to terms with the past have come under the framework of *Aufarbeitung der Vergangenheit* or *Vergangenheitsbewältigung*. Do the rule of law, pluralism and tolerance have anything to do with how nations come to terms with their troubled pasts? (Ash 2001/2002: 38) If Spain is an example of a stabile democracy that chose not to immediately examine the Franco years, Germany is an example of the opposite: a seemingly relentless confrontation with the Nazi past and one of the most successful open democracies.

Questions such as whether to open or close communist-era archives are particularly relevant because they raise the question of the truthfulness of the files and the entire process of informing. Trials are an important part of criminal justice, but can also lead to revenge and theatrical drama. Likewise, lustration as a kind of ritual purging is structurally unable to deal with the complexity of particular situations. What seems to be the most balanced and beneficial for the long-term health of a democracy are historical commissions. By listening to witnesses, who have lived through both the periods of communism and National Socialism, as well as interpreting archival material, a fuller understanding of the past may be reached. Moreover, historical commissions present a greater possibility for finding a balance between the sacralization and trivialization of memory.

For Ash, the issue of how memory is related to democracy basically boils down to four questions: whether, when, who and how (Ash 2002). The first, and probably most important question is *whether* one should address the past at all or simply ignore it. Before addressing the subtleties of how much or little to remember, one has to address whether it is beneficial to recall the past or whether amnesia and a 'new beginning' foster a peaceful society. Is it better to remember everything or 'forgive and forget?' Historically, the aim of a shared future has often resulted in state-sponsored forgetfulness. As early as 403 BC, with the restoration of Athenian democracy after oligarchy and civil war, amnesia was declared as a way in which to prevent revenge and promote reconciliation. Moreover, the Athenians installed an altar to Lethe, the goddess of forgetfulness on the acropolis as a sign that forgetfulness is necessary for a new beginning (Misztal 2005: 1324, Connerton 2008: 61-62). The Treaty of Westphalia ending the Thirty Years War in 1648 included an injunction that both sides should forgive and forget. When Charles II became king of England in 1660 he declared 'an act of full and general pardon, indemnity and oblivion' (Connerton 2008: 62). For Ernst Renan, national cohesion requires both shared memories and a certain degree of forgetfulness. 'Yet the essence of a nation is that all individuals have many things in common, and also that they have forgotten many things' (Renan 1990: 11). Indeed if one considers the liberal idea of the social contract, whether in the form of Thomas Hobbes or John Rawls, a period of willed forgetfulness is deemed necessary for future social cohesion. As Winston Churchill proclaimed in his 1946 Zurich speech, if Europe is to recover from the horror of war, a 'blessed act of oblivion' would be necessary. Such oblivion shouldn't conflict with the pursuit of justice, but instead prevent a vicious cycle of revenge and violence. 'If Europe is to be saved from infinite misery, and indeed from final doom, there must be this act of faith in the European family, this act of oblivion against all crimes and follies of the past' (Churchill 1946). From the opposite perspective, Karl Jaspers makes a powerful argument for the necessity to remember. In his book written immediately after the war, *The Question of German Guilt*, Jaspers outlines levels of individual guilt. Due to the crimes committed during National Socialism, each individual has a responsibility to remember—the issue becomes what kind of guilt is associated with the past: criminal, political, moral or metaphysical (Jaspers 1961). The democratic revolutions in Eastern Europe have been a watershed in claims for memory rather than forgetting. From the building of monuments and history museums, the writing of history books, films and documentaries to the academic discipline of memory studies, more memory seems to equal more democracy.

The second question that Ash raises is that of timing. *When* should the past be dealt with: immediately, in the near future or at some later time in the distant future. The question of timing is notoriously political because it implicates most directly those who served in the old regime. Thinkers, such as Hermann Lübbe suggest that a certain period of silence is necessary for democratic stability (Lübbe 2007). Without arguing for a magical amount of time, Lübbe cautions against disturbing the fragile texture of a new democracy with meddlesome questions about the past. German democratic stability is rooted in the official silence of the 1950s. Lübbe makes the compelling argument that future unity is more important that the seductive lure of revenge, scapegoats, and witch hunts. Here the argument to wait is as old as the adage that one should wait before reacting in a rash moment of anger. In essence, rational reflection requires a certain period of silence. In essence, 'time heals all wounds.' From the opposite spectrum, political thinkers such as Gesine Schwan argue that silence may just as easily be construed as justice postponed, amnesty or amnesia. Silence damages the political culture of a fragile democracy not only in the current generation but in future ones as well. Not acknowledging the past immediately results in silenced guilt (Schwan 2001). Thinkers who argue against waiting to confront the past harken back to a Freudian model of repression and the return of the repressed if the past is not immediately confronted. If not adequately acknowledged or dealt with, the past haunts and distorts the present and the future. From the point of view of historical scholarship, waiting limits what one can research. 'The witnesses die; others forget, or at least, rearrange their memories; and it is the worst horrors that are often the least well documented in the archives' (Ash 2002: 268).

The third question is *who* should judge the past: the leaders of the new democratic government, ordinary citizens, the international community, the media, parliament or the victims? Who should judge raises difficult moral questions of acceptance, mercy and forgiveness. Should those without experience living in a totalitarian regime judge the crimes of communism?

> What right have we, who never faced the dilemmas of living in a dictatorship, to sit in judgement on those who did? Do we know how we would have behaved? Perhaps we, too, would have become party functionaries or secret police informers? So what right do we have to condemn? (Ash 2002: 270)

Given the complexity of the communist dictatorship and totalitarian experience of living under both Nazism and communism, the question of 'who' should judge the past is linked to historical truth and justice. A lasting legacy of the war and communism in the Baltic States are the demographic changes resulting in large Russian-speaking minorities. As the riots surrounding the removal of the Bronze Soldier in Tallinn demonstrated, clashing memories are most volatile when linked to ethnic differences. If May 9 is remembered as a sacred day of victory for many Russians living in the Baltic States, it is marred by loss and occupation for many Lithuanians, Latvians and Estonians. Likewise the fact that the governments of Lithuania and Estonia chose not to attend the ceremonies commemorating the 60th anniversary of Victory Day in Moscow on May 9, 2005 revealed splits in how 'the end' of the war was remembered, interpreted and judged.

Finally, there is the question of *how* the past should be examined and judged: through trials, purges or history lessons. Each way has its own strength and weakness. Moreover, each path is dependent upon the countries transition to democracy. Ranging from the Nuremberg trials to Czech lustration and the East German Commission of Enquiry, the results are varied. Truth and History Commissions offer the most neutrality and greatest potential to learn about how regimes maintained power. For Ash, the most neutral judge of the past is the historian, rather than the politician or criminal judge. 'In fact I do think that if you ask "who is best equipped to do justice to the past?" the answer is, or at least should be, historians. But this is also a heavy responsibility' (Ash 2002: 281). Partially in response to international criticism about the lack of knowledge of war crimes and in an earnest attempt to document publicly recent history, each of the

Baltic States established historical commissions in the 1990s to investigate the Nazi and Communist occupations. The work of these commissions may, like the Entquete Commission in the former GDR (1995), provide a forthright historical analysis of the communist regime and post-war years. Although the Estonian commission is criticized for being more of a positivist fact-finding commission than providing in-depth historical analysis, it is the first attempt by Estonian historians in an international commission to examine the legacies of the war and occupations in Estonia. As Ash notes, historical commissions are one important way to understand the past. They complement trials, monuments, public debates, documentaries and the academic writing of history (Ash 2002: 265-282).

Uniqueness of Memory: Interpreting and Internalizing the Past

If, for Maurice Halbwachs, all memory is influenced by social frameworks, it is later with the work of Pierre Nora that the fascination with memory is linked to transformations in modern time (Halbwachs 1980, Nora 1989). In addition to calling attention to the locality of memory with his phrase 'place of memory' (*lieu de mémoire*), Nora emphasizes the cultural and mythical power of memory. 'This upsurge in memory intersects, it seems to me, with two major historical phenomena which have marked the age, one temporal and one social' (Nora 2002: 4). The first major transformation is a perceived acceleration of time. Modernity is more about rapid change than permanence, whether scientific, technological, social or political. In the quest for some place of certainty within an ever-accelerating world, people look towards the past for stability. Uncertainty towards a future where today's know-how may already be obsolete makes the past appear more stabile. The acceleration of time has two opposing consequences: either the past appears more stabile than the present and future, or the present is dramatically distanced from the past because it seemingly has nothing to do with the present. As a result of the closeness or distance of the past, the word 'memory' seems to have taken on a life of its own. '"Memory" has taken on meaning so broad and all-inclusive that it tends to be used purely and simply as a substitute for "history" and to put the study of history at the service of memory' (Nora 2002: 5). In addition to the acceleration of time, the upsurge in memory is also linked to the democratization of history. Merging with identity politics of minority groups and history from below, one consequence of the democratization of memory is a plurality of memories. 'Unlike history, which has always been in the hands of the public authorities, of scholars and specialized peer groups; memory has acquired all the new privileges of a popular protest movement' (Ibid., 7).

In response to the growing use of the term 'collective memory,' Reinhart Koselleck and Susan Sontag both argue *against* the salience of collective memory. For them, memory is an individual experience. At a conference held in Sofia in 2003 on the work of Pierre Nora, Koselleck presented a paper with the provocative thesis that there is no such thing as collective memory. Given his background as a historian and his own experience as a German soldier in a Soviet prisoner of war camp, Koselleck cautioned against the alluring confusion of collective memory. 'I can only remember what I myself have experienced. Memory (*Erinnerung*) is bound up with personal experience' (Koselleck 2004: 3). His memory of seeing Auschwitz from the first-hand perspective of a prisoner of war was different from the official commemorations of its liberation. 'As commemoration, as *re-commemoration*, it is semantically a fully different memory from that which I have kept in my memory as a witness from the initial news' (Ibid., 3). The collectivities that shape individual memory can be party, class, nation, union, religion—all the way up to the category of humanity. For Koselleck though, the question remains who is the subject, who remembers? The subject is the individual who may be influenced by what he terms 'the 7Ps': professors, priests, preachers, PR specialists, the press, poets and politicians (Ibid., 5). The seven groups in society simplify, mediate and define the terms of memory. 'There are as many memories as there are people and each collectivity, who is convinced that they are the only one, is, in my opinion, *a priori* ideology or myth' (Ibid., 6). In his opinion, there is no collective memory in the singular, but rather collective conditions that enable memory. 'There is no collective memory; there are collective conditions which make memory possible' (Ibid.). The role of the historian is not to support collective identity, but to try and understand the complexity of the past.

In a similar vein, Susan Sontag argues for the uniqueness of memory. Unlike Koselleck, who focuses on historical documents, Sontag bases her reflections on photography and art. Photography has the power to reduce the complexity of history into a single iconic image. She cautions against the facile equation of a photograph with historical truth. If memory is viewed in the singular, the complexity of human experience and the importance of culture are ignored. Interesting enough, while Sontag argues that 'strictly speaking, there is not such thing as collective memory,' (Sontag 2003: 85) Halbwachs insists on the opposite. For him, there is no such thing as a strictly individual memory; rather memory is always framed by membership in a group. 'In reality, we are never alone. Other men need not be physically present, since we always carry with us and in us a number of distinct persons' (Halbwachs 1980: 23). Culture, tradition and language are frameworks within which individual memories are located. Even if we experience something in private—like getting lost or taking a walk alone, the knowledge of the absent framework—be they smaller groups such as friends and family or larger groups like the nation—this knowledge of the absence of a group, constitutes a framework in absentia. 'The thought of the absent family provides a framework...' (Ibid., 38) Likewise, for Halbwachs, '... it is individuals *as group members* (*sic*) who remember' (Ibid., 48). All memories are framed by some form of social collectivity—be it the family, religion or nation. It is only when we dream that Halbwachs admits some form of private and individual memory.

Both Sontag and Koselleck share a similar concern with the emphasis on 'collective memory.' Just as guilt is individual, so is memory. One should be careful of projecting individual experience onto collectivities. However, even if memory is private, one can and should learn from the larger processes of history. 'All memory is individual, unreproducible – it dies with each person' (Sontag 2003: 86). Collective instruction means the internalization of the past and acknowledgment of some sort of responsibility for past actions. Responsibility, unlike guilt can be collective and between generations. Likewise, collective instruction includes historical research, discussion and critical debate. The trick seems to be in distinguishing between collective instruction as education and collective instruction as ideology. If memory becomes frozen or rendered into a mythical image, it is difficult to think about. Likewise, memories of events are only the beginning, not the end of understanding.

Mesomemory: Between Sacralization and Trivialization

Contemporary historians such as Tony Judt, Norman Davies, Anne Appelbaum and Timothy Snyder argue for the importance of a balance within European memory. Too much memory can lead to endless conflict and myth, while too little memory engenders ignorance and the possible falsification of history. They argue for more research into former communist countries during both the years of National Socialism and communism. 1989 looks back not only to 1945 but, to Hitler's rise to power in 1933. Since the experiences of 1945-1989 were dramatically different in East and West, Snyder calls for a balancing of the books. If the starting point of a common European narrative is the desire for peace after 1945 and the beginning of the European project, 1945 for Eastern Europe marked the replacement of one occupation with another. 'The absence of a common European historical narrative, embracing both east and west, leads to failures of understanding and solidarity... The future of European solidarity, in other words, depends on a rethinking of the immediate European past' (Snyder 2005). For him, two issues have to be rethought: recognition that the center of suffering was in the East not the West and that for two generations, Eastern Europeans did not experience European integration, but communism. Given the different experiences in Europe, a common understanding of the recent past is complex. At the moment, three major narratives seem to co-exist: a Western narrative emphasizing the centrality of the Holocaust and Nazism, an Eastern narrative emphasizing national suffering under double occupations and deportations and a Soviet/Russian narrative remembering the victory of the Soviet Union over Nazi fascism and the suffering of the Russian people.

In *Memory and Hope*, Tzvetan Todorov discusses the lessons one might learn from the totalitarian regimes of the twentieth century. 'Totalitarianism now belongs to the past; that particular disease has been beaten. But we need to understand what happened. As noted by Zhelieu Zhelev, a former dissident who was briefly president of Bulgaria: *before turning a page, you need to read it (sic)*' (Todorov 2003: 6). In order to understand how totalitarianism emerged and remained firmly in place until 1989 in Eastern Europe and 1991 in the USSR, one has to examine the past. Cast within his larger critique of modernity, Todorov focuses on the fragility of humanity. Going against the grain of contemporary cynicism, hedonistic individualism and a general sense of hopelessness, he seeks to remember moments of humanity within the barbarism of totalitarianism. The question is not whether one should remember or forget, but *how* to internalize possible lessons for the future of Europe. If the page of history is turned too quickly, one doesn't have time to read and reflect on the complexity of historical events. Todorov cautions wisely for a more measured memory: one that does not give into the extremes of sacralization or trivialization. Once a memory is made sacred, one cannot question or compare it with anything else. Instead it becomes an icon removed from ordinary time. Likewise, if images of suffering are repeated too often, the effect might be one of numbing indifference. 'It is hard to find the path that skirts the pitfalls of sanctification and of trivialization that leads us neither to serve only our interest nor to give lessons only to others. But that strait and narrow path does exist' (Ibid., 176).

Perhaps part of the difficulty resides in the either/or framework. Since memory involves selection and partial forgetfulness, the either/or dichotomy is misleading. Not everything can be remembered. Instead of *either* memory *or* forgetting, one might consider Ash's discussion of amnesia, hypermemory, and a middle memory (Ash 2001). The term hypermemory (*hypermnesie*), coined by Alain Besançon denotes the injunction 'never to forget' and the uniqueness of the Holocaust (Besançon 2001). Hypermemory views the past as a trauma to be continually remembered. Amnesia is forgetting: the conscious blocking out of events and phases. Since both hypermemory and amnesia are extremes, Ash pleas for a more modest form of memory that is situated between the poles of total memory and complete forgetting. Mesomemory (*mesomnesie*) is a middle memory that seeks to learn from the past as well as to put the past behind. Mesomemory does not see the present eternally through the eyes of the past. Likewise, Ash's middle memory recognizes the past, but doesn't stay fixated within the traumatic moment. Mesomemory is akin to Nietzsche's plea for a balance between the historical and unhistorical. The emphasis is on how to live peacefully together in the present. Likewise, Ash's memory is similar to Todorov's memory that goes between sacralization and trivialization. What Ash makes very clear though with his historical discussion of state-sponsored memory and forgetting is that memory alone is unable to guarantee democracy. The balance between memory and forgetting, the historical and unhistorical is a slippery slope. In a similar spirit, Barbara Misztal argues that memory alone is not a sufficient condition for democracy. 'It appears that what matters for democracy's health is not social remembering per se but *the way* (*sic*) in which the past is called up and used' (Misztal 2005: 1336). Memory, like imagination has a certain plasticity that can fade or increase in mythological importance with the passing of time.

When memory gains a kind of 'sacred status,' it hinders historians from critical research. Instead there is a greater tendency towards stereotypes and myth (Misztal 2004, 2005). Particularly when discussion focuses on the victims of communism and Nazism, the psychoanalytic framework of individual trauma is often cast onto the wider collective of society or nation. One of the ways that 1989 is linked to 1945 is the close relation between a traumatic past and democratic renewal. Since the Nuremberg trials, interpreting the past as a burden to be worked through and internalized has become a feature of democratization. Indeed, the two are linked together because the recognition and internalization of a difficult past has the possibility to strengthen a democracy. When the past however is used as a political weapon or for reasons of revenge, memory can weaken rather than strengthen a fledging democracy.

While individuals may agree on freedom as a beautiful ideal, it is democracy as a way of life and the uncertainty of living in an open society that proves to be the most difficult. Freedom can bring uncertainty, rather than stability. The question of how citizens in democratic nations *should* come to terms with difficult pasts puts a new twist on one of the oldest questions of social justice: 'Am I my brother's keeper?'. Cain's question of whether we, as individuals bear any responsibility for others is still a fundamental question of the human condition. Responses from trials, purges, truth commissions, national apologies, relocation of monuments, and the re-writing of history books are all different ways of linking responsibility for past deeds to the present community. The democratic response to a difficult past is yes; we should be our brother's keeper. But who is defined as a brother, and how individuals decide to link together as a community balanced between the past and the future is a politically charged and delicate answer.

References

Adorno, T. 1986. What Does Coming to Terms with the Past Mean?, trans. Geoffrey Hartman, in *Bitburg in Moral and Political Perspective*. Indianapolis, IN: Indiana University Press, 114-129.
Appelbaum, A. 2003. *Gulag: A History*. New York: Penguin Books.
Ash, T.G. 2001/2002. Mesomnesie: Pläydoyer für ein mittleres Erinnern. *Transit*, Winter, 32-48.
Ash, T.G. 2002. Trials, Purges and History Lessons: Treating a Difficult Past in Post-Communist Europe in *Memory and Power in Post-War Europe*, edited by Jan-Werner Müller. Cambridge: Cambridge University Press, 265-282.
Bescançon, A. 2001. *Sajandi Õnnetus: Kommunismist, Natsismist ja Holokausti Ainulaadsusest*, trans. Katre Talviste. Tallinn: Loomingu Raamutukogu.
Churchill, W. 1946. Speech given 19 September 1946 at Zurich University. Available at http://www.jef.at/cms/wp-content/uploads/churchill.pdf. Accessed November 10, 2009.
Connerton, P. 2008. Seven Types of Forgetting. *Memory Studies*, 1:1, 59-71.
Davies, N. 2006. *Europe at War: 1939-1945. No Simple Victory*. London: Pan Books.

Halbwachs, M. 1980 (1950). *The Collective Memory*, trans. Francis J. Ditter, Jr. and Vida Yazdi Ditter. New York: Harper Colophon.
Halbwachs, M. 1992 (1941). *On Collective Memory*, trans. Lewis A. Coser. Chicago, IL: University of Chicago Press.
Jaspers, K. 1961 (1947). *The Question of German Guilt*, trans. E.B. Ashton. New York: Capricorn Books.
Judt, T. 2002. The Past is Another Country: Myth and Memory in Post-war Europe, in *Memory and Power in Post-War Europe*, edited by Jan-Werner Müller. Cambridge: Cambridge University Press, 157-183.
Judt, T. 2005. *Postwar: A History of Europe since 1945*. New York: Penguin Press.
Koselleck, R. 2004. Gibt es ein kollektives Gedächtnis? *Divinatio*, 19:2, Spring, 1-6.
Lübbe, H. 2007. *Von Parteigenossen zum Bundesbürger: Über beschweigene und historische Vergangenheiten*. Wilhelm Fink.
Misztal, B. 2004. The Sacralization of Memory. *European Journal of Social Theory*, 7:1, 67-84.
Misztal, B. 2005. Memory and Democracy. *American Behavioral Scientist*. 48:10, June, 1320-1338.
Nietzsche, F. 1980 (1874). *On the Advantage and Disadvantage of History for Life*, trans. Peter Preuss. Indianapolis, IN: Hackett Publishing.
Nora, P. 1989. Between Memory and History: Les Lieux de Mémoire. *Representations*, 26, Spring: 7-25.
Nora, P. 2002. Reasons for the Current Upsurge in Memory. *Transit*, 4. Available at www.eurozine.com. Accessed 13 March, 2009.
Renan, E. 1990. What is a Nation?, in *Nation and Narration*. New York: Routledge, 8-22.
Schwan, G. 2001. *Politics and Guilt: The Destructive Power of Silence*, trans. Thomas Dunlap. Lincoln, NE: University of Nebraska Press.
Snyder, T. 2005. Balancing the Books. *Index on Censorship*, Number 2. Available at www.eurozine.com. Accessed November 11, 2009.
Snyder, T. 2010. *Bloodlands: Europe Between Hitler and Stalin*. New York: Basic Books.
Sontag, S. 2003. *Regarding the Pain of Others*. New York: Picador.
Todorov, T. 2003. *Hope and Memory: Reflections on the Twentieth Century*. London: Atlantic Books.

and Nazism, the psychoanalytic framework of individual trauma is often cast onto the wider collective of society or nation. One of the ways that 1989 is linked to 1945 is the close relation between a traumatic past and democratic renewal. Since the Nuremberg trials, interpreting the past as a burden to be worked through and internalized has become a feature of democratization. Indeed, the two are linked together because the recognition and internalization of a difficult past has the possibility to strengthen a democracy. When the past however is used as a political weapon or for reasons of revenge, memory can weaken rather than strengthen a fledging democracy.

While individuals may agree on freedom as a beautiful ideal, it is democracy as a way of life and the uncertainty of living in an open society that proves to be the most difficult. Freedom can bring uncertainty, rather than stability. The question of how citizens in democratic nations *should* come to terms with difficult pasts puts a new twist on one of the oldest questions of social justice: 'Am I my brother's keeper?'. Cain's question of whether we, as individuals bear any responsibility for others is still a fundamental question of the human condition. Responses from trials, purges, truth commissions, national apologies, relocation of monuments, and the re-writing of history books are all different ways of linking responsibility for past deeds to the present community. The democratic response to a difficult past is yes; we should be our brother's keeper. But who is defined as a brother, and how individuals decide to link together as a community balanced between the past and the future is a politically charged and delicate answer.

References

Adorno, T. 1986. What Does Coming to Terms with the Past Mean?, trans. Geoffrey Hartman, in *Bitburg in Moral and Political Perspective*. Indianapolis, IN: Indiana University Press, 114-129.
Appelbaum, A. 2003. *Gulag: A History*. New York: Penguin Books.
Ash, T.G. 2001/2002. Mesomnesie: Pläydoyer für ein mittleres Erinnern. *Transit*, Winter, 32-48.
Ash, T.G. 2002. Trials, Purges and History Lessons: Treating a Difficult Past in Post-Communist Europe in *Memory and Power in Post-War Europe*, edited by Jan-Werner Müller. Cambridge: Cambridge University Press, 265-282.
Besçançon, A. 2001. *Sajandi Õnnetus: Kommunismist, Natsismist ja Holokausti Ainulaadsusest*, trans. Katre Talviste. Tallinn: Loomingu Raamutukogu.
Churchill, W. 1946. Speech given 19 September 1946 at Zurich University. Available at http://www.jef.at/cms/wp-content/uploads/churchill.pdf. Accessed November 10, 2009.
Connerton, P. 2008. Seven Types of Forgetting. *Memory Studies*, 1:1, 59-71.
Davies, N. 2006. *Europe at War: 1939-1945. No Simple Victory*. London: Pan Books.

Halbwachs, M. 1980 (1950). *The Collective Memory*, trans. Francis J. Ditter, Jr. and Vida Yazdi Ditter. New York: Harper Colophon.
Halbwachs, M. 1992 (1941). *On Collective Memory*, trans. Lewis A. Coser. Chicago, IL: University of Chicago Press.
Jaspers, K. 1961 (1947). *The Question of German Guilt*, trans. E.B. Ashton. New York: Capricorn Books.
Judt, T. 2002. The Past is Another Country: Myth and Memory in Post-war Europe, in *Memory and Power in Post-War Europe*, edited by Jan-Werner Müller. Cambridge: Cambridge University Press, 157-183.
Judt, T. 2005. *Postwar: A History of Europe since 1945*. New York: Penguin Press.
Koselleck, R. 2004. Gibt es ein kollektives Gedächtnis? *Divinatio*, 19:2, Spring, 1-6.
Lübbe, H. 2007. *Von Parteigenossen zum Bundesbürger: Über beschweigene und historische Vergangenheiten*. Wilhelm Fink.
Misztal, B. 2004. The Sacralization of Memory. *European Journal of Social Theory*, 7:1, 67-84.
Misztal, B. 2005. Memory and Democracy. *American Behavioral Scientist*. 48:10, June, 1320-1338.
Nietzsche, F. 1980 (1874). *On the Advantage and Disadvantage of History for Life*, trans. Peter Preuss. Indianapolis, IN: Hackett Publishing.
Nora, P. 1989. Between Memory and History: Les Lieux de Mémoire. *Representations*, 26, Spring: 7-25.
Nora, P. 2002. Reasons for the Current Upsurge in Memory. *Transit*, 4. Available at www.eurozine.com. Accessed 13 March, 2009.
Renan, E. 1990. What is a Nation?, in *Nation and Narration*. New York: Routledge, 8-22.
Schwan, G. 2001. *Politics and Guilt: The Destructive Power of Silence*, trans. Thomas Dunlap. Lincoln, NE: University of Nebraska Press.
Snyder, T. 2005. Balancing the Books. *Index on Censorship*, Number 2. Available at www.eurozine.com. Accessed November 11, 2009.
Snyder, T. 2010. *Bloodlands: Europe Between Hitler and Stalin*. New York: Basic Books.
Sontag, S. 2003. *Regarding the Pain of Others*. New York: Picador.
Todorov, T. 2003. *Hope and Memory: Reflections on the Twentieth Century*. London: Atlantic Books.

Chapter 2
Agreeing to Disagree on the Legacies of Recent History

Since 1989 social change in Europe has moved between two familiar stories. The first being a politics of memory emphasizing the specificity of culture in national narratives and the other extolling the virtues of the Enlightenment heritage of reason and humanity. The tension between unique culture and common humanity can be found in the various ways that World War II has been remembered after the fall of the Berlin Wall and the break-up of the Soviet Union. Rifts between old and new Europe are visible with the renewed efforts by the East European countries and the Baltic States for official recognition of communist crimes at the European Union level and hesitancy on the part of old Europe for such official recognition. In the wake of heated debates surrounding the 60th commemoration of Victory Day in Moscow (2005) and the Soviet war memorial controversy in Tallinn (2007), a common understanding of World War II and the Cold War that divided the continent is far from reached (Petersoo and Tamm 2008, Onken 2007a).

While the Holocaust forms a central part of West European collective memory, national victimhood of former communist countries tends to occlude the centrality of the Holocaust. Do attempts to find one single European memory of victimhood ignore the complexity of history and denigrate those who suffered under communism and National Socialism? Is there a way to respect historical difference without revisionism and a whitewashing of the past? How might different European nations remember the past without fixating too much on difference? These questions are particularly relevant in the Baltic States and Eastern Europe, where citizens were under double occupations of Nazi Germany and the USSR during and after World War II. Without arguing for relativism, pluralism in the sense of Hannah Arendt and Isaiah Berlin is presented as a way in which to move beyond the settling of scores in the past and towards a respectful recognition and acknowledgment of historical difference. Agreeing to disagree includes respect for multiple memories, recognition of cultural difference and empathy with others. Because relations between Russia and the Baltic States have been antagonistic and the memories of World War II tend to exclude one another, it is not likely that they can agree to disagree until Russia as the successor state to the Soviet Union recognizes the crimes of communism. Old and new Europe though can agree to disagree because both sides acknowledge a plurality of historical experiences during the Second World War.

Legacies of History: The Past as Inheritance and Burden

A legacy can be interpreted as both negative and positive, as both an inheritance and a burden. Stemming from the Latin *legatus*, a legacy means 'something transmitted by or received from an ancestor or predecessor from the past.' It is this two-fold meaning of legacy as inheritance and burden that I discuss, first theoretically and then with respect to different narratives about World War II since 1989. My reflections on the East European experience draw primarily from the Baltic case of Estonia. Occupied by both the Soviet Union (1940-1941, 1944-1991) and Nazi Germany (1941-1944), Estonia provides a kind of microcosm for clashing memories of the war and its legacy.

Before memory studies became a subject of academic interest, the older school of hermeneutics highlighted the importance of interpretation and understanding. Indeed, it is from the perspective of hermeneutics that the historical importance of a legacy first becomes salient. As Hans-Georg Gadamer argued in *Truth and Method*, one can never truly free oneself from the cultural traditions and prejudices that one is born into.

> In fact history does not belong to us; we belong to it. Long before we understand ourselves through the process of self-examination, we understand ourselves in a self-evident way in the family, society, and state in which we live. The self-awareness of the individual is only a flickering in the closed circuits of historical life. *That is why the prejudices of the individual, far more than his judgments, constitute the historical reality of his being.* (Gadamer 1975: 277)

Hermeneutics highlights understanding and what Gadamer calls, effective historical consciousness. 'Consciousness of being affected by history (*wirkungsgeschichtliches Bewusstsein*) is primarily consciousness of the hermeneutical situation' (Gadamer 1975: 301). The effects of history are legacies of the past that are meaningful in the present. One can never totally free oneself from the past and be a purely rational being, neither is one condemned to reproduce blindly the prejudices of one's tradition. The individual has the potential to criticize and evaluate his or her own traditions. In this sense, World War II and its legacy are deeply part of contemporary European society. Each person has a finite but changing horizon of understanding. '*To be historically means that knowledge of oneself can never be complete*' (Gadamer 1975: 302). Understanding is a kind of dialog whereby we try to put ourselves in the perspective of the other person. There is no universal common horizon but rather many changing perspectives.

> In fact the horizon of the present is continually in the process of being formed because we are continually having to test all our prejudices. An important point of this testing occurs in encountering the past and in understanding the tradition from which we come. Hence the horizon of the present cannot be formed without the past. (Gadamer 1975: 306)

A legacy entails links between past, present and future. Something from the past is remembered and influences actions in the present. For Koselleck, a contemporary of Gadamer, the metaphor of horizon applies more to the future than to the past. He refers to the 'space of experience' and the 'horizon of expectation.' The past is constituted spatially, as a kind of map or place in which experiences have been completed. The future is qualitatively different because it is open to the unknown and has not yet been experienced.

> Hope and memory, or expressed more generally, expectation and experience – for expectation comprehends more than hope, and experience goes deeper than memory – simultaneously constitute history and its cognition. They do so by demonstrating and producing the inner relation between past and future earlier, today, or tomorrow. (Koselleck 1985: 270)

While Gadamer and Koselleck emphasize the historical aspect of human understanding, it is in the work of Paul Ricoeur that imagination and narrative are brought into the picture. What links the space of experience with the horizon of expectation is imagination. Mnemosyne is the goddess of both memory and imagination, as well as the mother of Clio or history. Recollection of the past is not a static re-capturing of an event but a fluid even imaginative activity. Ricoeur calls attention to 'social imaginaries.' The social imaginary, similar to Anderson's 'imagined community' are those collective stories, histories and ideologies that inform our understanding. Ricoeur highlights the central link between narrative and time. It is through narrative that a sense of time is experienced. 'A story is *made of* events, to the extent that plot makes events *into* a story' (Ricoeur 1991: 106). Each narrative has a plot that structures the development of a story—be it fact or fiction. A plot gives both a narrative order and meaning to what might otherwise be construed as haphazard and disconnected.

Halbwachs and Nora reveal how the legacy of the past becomes a politics of memory in contemporary societies. Rather than emphasizing a clear-cut distinction between past and present, the link between past and present is foregrounded. In his pioneering work, Halbwachs argued that memory is framed by membership in different social groups. Individuals remember as social beings living in particular time periods and belonging to certain generations. Nora's interdisciplinary study of the topography of memory or *lieu de mémoire* calls attention to the symbolic places where memory is represented (Nora 1989: 1996). The wave of semiotics, cultural studies and influence of history from below marked a shift from a philosophical analysis of interpretation to an analysis of the symbolic production and reception of cultural phenomena. Thus, places of memory include not only physical spaces such as monuments, museums, film and literature, but also temporal places such as commemorative ceremonies (Connerton 1989). Studies of oral history, post-colonialism, histories from below and of histories of everyday life offer different perspectives and narratives about the past. Multiculturalism and attention to ways in which national and ethnic identity are shaped is deeply part of the democratization of history. Categories such 'memory' and 'culture' have become the subjects of academic interest, replacing 'society' or 'class.' Peter Burke carefully points out that since the 1970s culture has replaced society in both academic and popular literature (Burke 2004: 65-66). In a similar vein, Alon Confino argues that memory has replaced society as a social category for understanding collective behavior. Both are right because memories of the past are a part of the larger sphere of culture— of symbols and their interpretation (Confino 2006: 170-188). It is this cultural approach to the past that interprets museums, monuments and commemorations as meaningful symbols linked to collective identity that is of issue in the last 20 years (Burke 2004: 3).

Recent interest in collective memory is furthermore linked to a moral acknowledgment of the Holocaust as the central trauma of the twentieth century. Before the Holocaust, legacies of the past were examined less as burdens and more as tradition, heritage or inheritance. Even Nietzsche's provocative writings on history did not discuss the past as traumatic burden. The past becomes a burden when it prevents the individual from living in the present. Whether seen as monumental, antiquarian or critical—the greatness of the past becomes a burden when it eclipses the present and the future. Halbwachs also focused on the social frameworks of memory in a neutral way. Likewise, although Anderson's seminal *Imagined Communities* harkened back to Ernst Renan's famous remark that it is shared sorrows rather than joys that unites nations—it was not yet the language of trauma and mourning (Anderson 1991). The nation as imagined community was still within the framework of collective identity as a kind of cohesion and solidarity between individuals. Here tradition, symbols, heritage movements and commemorative rituals were examined without reference to questions of justice and trauma (Lowenthal 1985, Nora 1996, Hobsbawm 1983, Shils 1981). The legacy of the past was viewed as a meaningful inheritance rather than as a traumatic burden.

The democratization of history and emergence of transitional justice in the late twentieth century accompanies the examination of traumatic pasts (Alexander et al., 2004, Bell 2006, Giesen 2004). By emphasizing the past as trauma, three concepts are intertwined: memory, democracy and justice. According to Jeffrey K. Olick, the past can either be discussed as presentist, functional or psychoanalytic. While the presentist understanding of the past is about 'what *we* do *with* the past,' and privileges the instrumental control of the past from the point of view of the present, the functional understanding of the past imploys a moral tone by asking, 'what the *past* does *for* us.' Here the past is the moral-political source of individual and collective identity. It is the understanding of the past as trauma that has become increasingly prevalent. The Freudian model of psychoanalysis interprets the legacy of the past in terms of a burden: 'what the past does *to* us' (Olick 2007b).

What happens when the individual model of trauma is projected onto collectivities such as the nation or Western civilization as a whole? Does the metaphor foster complexities and distortions? Can the question 'what does the past do to us?' coincide with another relevant question 'how to come to terms with the past?' In other words, how is the traumatic model of individual memory from the psychoanalytical side, incorporating mourning, melancholia, repression and repetition linked to that other moral-political model of trauma (*Vergangenheitsbewältingung* and *Aufarbeitung der Vergangenheit*)? Adorno's famous essay 'What Does Coming to Terms with the Past Mean?' (1959) and Karl Jasper's *The Question of German Guilt* written immediately after the war are attempts to understand the legacy of National Socialism for those who lived through the years 1933-1945. Adorno argued strongly for the centrality of Freudian psychology when dealing with the past. 'The need for an exact and undiluted knowledge of Freudian theory is as imperative as ever' (Adorno 1986: 127).

If the psychoanalytical model seems to unwittingly privilege a passive conception of the person—*what the past does to us*—the moral-political model of working through the past leaves open the possibility for a more active conception of the person. The model of *Aufarbeitung* is one of working through, coming to terms with, mastery, overcoming, in essence, acceptance and acknowledgement of the past-present link. It begins from trauma but does not remain fixated on it. Concepts such as the past as a burden, inheritance and legacy gain a new meaning when they are *not only* viewed from the psychoanalytic perspective. If trauma is the singular hallmark of our times, is there room for individuals to learn from their mistakes and take responsibility for the legacy of past wrongdoings. Is not the very recognition of trauma linked to justice and pluralism? (Minow 1998, Olick 2007a). Regret indicates individual action and the freedom of the will. Regret and remorse indicate that individuals and perhaps even societies can learn from their past mistakes and assume responsibility for aspects of the past (Schwan 2001). Regret and responsibility are linked to the freedom of the individual to change. Whether told in the story of religious or individual change, the conversion of the spirit is deeply part of the Western tradition: from Saul to Paul, St. Augustine, and Dostoevsky's Raskolnikov—regret for past actions can lead to individual change and a new beginning.

While trauma is one powerful emblem of our times, one can also make a similar case for democracy. The two emblems are linked: the recognition of a traumatic past (as mourning, regret or guilt) seems to be a fundamental cornerstone of post-war democracy. Trauma and democracy are linked together as two sides of the same coin. The language of human rights after the Second World War with Nuremburg's precedent of 'crimes against humanity' has enriched democratic culture with emphasis on the recognition of difference and dignity of the human being. Continuing in the tradition of Jasper's distinction between different types of guilt as criminal, political, moral and metaphysical, Gesine Schwan has developed the thesis that guilt which is silenced or repressed damages the political culture of democracy (Schwan 2001). Return of the repressed occurs when guilt is silenced. Learning processes, individual and social change and, perhaps most importantly, trust are built during the difficult process of the acknowledgement of guilt. Schwan's work, like that of the Mitscherlich's and Bude is concerned with the dialogue between generations and democratic culture (Bude 1992, Mitscherlich and Mitscherlich 1975).

The relation between traumatic past and democratic renewal is what links 1989 to 1945. Interpreting the past as a burden to be acknowledged and worked through makes the very strong claim that the twentieth century or modernity itself is defined by trauma. 'Indeed, one could well argue that 'trauma' has become something of an emblem of our epoch' (Olick 2007a: 21). From Adorno, Bauman and Benjamin a tragic understanding of history is employed whereby Auschwitz becomes the emblem for a fundamental break in Western civilization (Adorno 1986, Bauman 1989, Benjamin, 1968, Friedländer 1992). The argument though runs into a paradox: either the Holocaust is removed from history into a realm of being beyond representation or one enters into the discussion of whether the Holocaust was more of a break in civilization than other mass genocides, most notably those of communism.

Narratives of the Second World War

In the hermeneutical spirit of Gadamer and Ricoeur, the Second World War serves as an example of the role of narrative in shaping different understandings of the past upon the present. Since the end of the war, three broad narratives have surfaced: a Western, a Soviet/Russian and (since 1989/1991) a post-Soviet/post-communist narrative. Each narrative highlights different aspects of the war that are factually true, but politically charged. Indeed, it is the way in which the legacies of the same war are remembered that makes the narratives so different (Lebow 2006). Each narrative is linked to national identity and collective suffering. Because the emergence of the mass media occurred at roughly the same time as the war, photographs, documentaries and film plays a pivotal role in the different interpretations of the Second World War. Contrasting iconic images of the war years are seared into the different stories of the years 1939-1945.

Western Narrative

The Western narrative of World War II highlights National Socialism as the main evil. The Holocaust is unique and the Jews of Europe represent trauma and victimhood. The war began on the September 1, 1939, when Hitler invaded Poland and ended on May 8th 1945 with the capitulation of Nazi Germany to the Allied powers. The defeat and division of Germany was the result of the war and of the ensuing Cold War that divided the continent. Even if both National Socialism and Stalinism may be viewed as totalitarian, the crimes of communism are generally regarded to be in a different category from those of the Holocaust. Although increasing attention has turned to the suffering of German civilians during the war, photographs of Jewish deportation and Nazi concentration camps remain the iconic symbols of the Second World War (Barnouw 2005, Sebald 2003, Grass, 2004, 2007). Indeed the very word 'Auschwitz' has become a central signifier for the Second World War. In addition to traditional war memorials, abstract monuments to genocide and the Holocaust are a part of the West European landscape. Particularly in Germany and Western Europe, the Western narrative of World War II is linked to a Habermasian conception of post-national identity and constitutional patriotism (Habermas 1993, 2001). In many ways, the Western narrative is a loose framework shared by Western Europe, the USA and Israel in which each nation has a slightly different approach to the narrative based upon national experience.

Soviet/Russian Narrative

In the Soviet/Russian narrative, fascism (National Socialism) is the undisputed main evil. The victimhood of the Russian people is remembered as the primary trauma against Nazi/fascist invasion. The Red Army soldier is a hero and liberator of Europe, not an occupier of Eastern Europe. The West tends to underestimate the heroism of the Red Army and enormous suffering of the Soviet people. The war is not remembered in Russia as World War II but as the Great Patriotic War. Beginning on June 22, 1941 with Operation Barbarossa, it ended on May 9, 1945 when Nazi Germany surrendered to the Soviet Union. The years 1939-1941 when the Soviet Union was allied with Nazi Germany are downplayed and not part of the official narrative of the Great Patriotic War. The numerous monuments to the war throughout the former Soviet Union emphasize victory, heroism and national sacrifice for the Motherland. The iconic symbol of the Soviet narrative is Khaldei's famous photograph of a Red Army soldier flying the Soviet flag over the Reichstag on May 9. There is a distinctive continuity in contemporary Russia with the Soviet narrative of the Great Patriotic War. The commemoration marking the 60th anniversary of the end of the war in 2005 demonstrated the central place of the Great Patriotic War in Russian national consciousness (Gudkov 2005). Furthermore the refusal of the Russian Federation to officially recognize the occupation of the Baltic States (1944-1991) is part of the story of the Soviet liberation of Europe.

Post-communist/Post-Soviet Narrative

In the post-communist/post-Soviet narrative there are two evils: communism and National Socialism; however, communism is widely regarded as the main evil by way of duration and intensity. National victimhood is the primary trauma that has been silenced during the Cold War occupation years. Particularly in the Baltics, the Holocaust is seen as peripheral to national suffering due to war and dual occupations. Both the Nazi and Red Army soldiers are viewed as occupiers. The real end of the war is neither May 8th nor May 9th, but the restoration of independence and end of Soviet occupation in 1991. The end of communism marks a return to history and a return to Europe. In the Baltics, it is the secret protocols of the Molotov-Ribbentrop pact on August 23, 1939 dividing Europe into spheres of influence between Hitler and Stalin that should not be forgotten.

Furthermore the dates of Soviet deportations of the Balts to Siberia and the Gulag in 1941 and 1949 are remembered in the national calendar much more than May 8 or 9. In Estonia, the national day of mourning (June 14) is officially dedicated to those who were deported and killed in the Gulag. The central iconic images of the war are of the Red Army and deportation (Kõresaar 2005).

Whereas one might argue that the genocide of European Jewry has been internalized into a post-national Western narrative about the Second World War, for the Soviet-Russian and post-Soviet perspective, the Holocaust is external to their national narratives of the same period of time: 1939-1945. While most West European countries experienced reconstruction and democratization after the war, the post-war experience of East Europeans, the Balts in particular, are more linked to occupation, deportation, and the demographic changes due to Soviet Russification policies.

The Legacies of War after 1989

Since 1989, there has been a reassessment of Western myths and grand narratives surrounding World War II and the entire post-war period. Historians such as Judt, Davies, Snyder, Beevor and Appelbaum have written forcefully about the way in which memories of the war have been used for political gains and to shore up national identities. Davies, Appelbaum and Snyder are particularly critical of Western ignorance and relative disinterest in the Eastern Front and the crimes of communism. While walking through Prague one summer day, Appelbaum asks why it is politically acceptable for Westerners to buy Soviet kitsch but morally reprehensible to indulge in Nazi paraphernalia.

> Most of the people buying the Soviet paraphernalia were Americans and West Europeans. All would be sickened by the thought of wearing a swastika. None objected, to wearing the hammer and sickle on a T-shirt or a hat. It was a minor observation, but sometimes it is through just such minor observations that a cultural mood is best observed. For here, the lesson could not have been clearer: while the symbol of one mass murder fills us with horror, the symbol of another mass murder makes us laugh. (Appelbaum 2003: 5-6)

Appelbaum's point is an important one. Symbols of communism seem to be taken lightly in the West, whereas symbols of National Socialism are considered sinister and taboo. Western narratives of the Second World War suffer from an unbalanced account privileging the Western Front and underestimating the crucial role of the Red Army in winning the war. Moreover the problem of criminality has 'been carefully avoided by Soviet apologists' (Davies 2006: 483).

The different memories of World War II in contemporary Europe are linked to important social changes since 1989. The first is generational. As Karl Mannheim argued, historical events mark the formative years of individuals so that generations share certain lived experiences that influence their values and sense of collective identity (Mannheim 1952). Memories of the past are linked to living members of a particular generation. Those with lived experience of the war are dying out and younger generations learn about the war and the Cold War through the cultural mediation of media, books, television, film and museums. Since the 1980s, a generational shift has been underway in which lived communicative memory is gradually being replaced by second-hand cultural memory (Assmann 1995). The 1990s and early 21st century are perhaps the twilight zone when communicative memory is being overshadowed by cultural memory.

The second major social change actually occurred before 1989 when the Holocaust became a topic both academically and popularly. Beginning in the 1960s and booming in the 1980s, memories of the Holocaust and Jewish suffering reached unprecedented proportions. Narratives of the Holocaust were and still are linked with moral questions of representation and justice. Indeed the general trend of examining traumatic pasts begins with the Holocaust. With the break-up of the Soviet Union and the fall of the Berlin Wall, the importance of the Holocaust as a central prism through which World War II is remembered has only increased.

Thirdly, the largely peaceful revolutions in Eastern Europe and the spectacular break-up of the Soviet Union have forever changed Europe. The largest experiment in social engineering creaked to an end. Yet, it is here that the legacies of history are most vibrant and the rate of social change most rapid (Outhwaite and Ray 2005: 176-196). What happened during these revolutions is important for many reasons. However, it is perhaps the legacy of what *didn't* happen that is now haunting Europe. Unlike the Second World War that ended with the controversial Nuremberg Trials, communism ended without official recognition of the crimes committed in the name of the Soviet Union. Moreover, the fact that Putin's government increasingly mythologized the Great Patriotic War prevents the very recognition of communist crimes that Nuremberg in its flawed way facilitated. While one might criticize the Nuremberg Trials as 'victors' justice' because only Nazi German crimes were prosecuted and Stalinist crimes and Allied bombing of civilians were ignored, Nuremberg did establish the important precedent of crimes against humanity and ushered in an era of human rights (Cooper 1999).

Comparing the Crimes of Communism and Nazism

In the Holocaust Forum held in Stockholm in 2000, the Holocaust was discussed as a central narrative of modernity.[1] Yehuda Bauer's speech summed up the main

---

1 In May 1998, the governments of Sweden, Britian and the United States established the Task Force for International Cooperation on Holocaust Education, Remembrance and Research. They were later joined by Germany, Israel, Poland, the Netherlands, France and Italy. The Stockholm International Forum took place January 26-28, 2000.

idea of the conference, 'In recent decades, actually in most recent years, we have witnessed an amazing development. A catastrophe that had befallen a specific people at a specific time, in a specific place, has been accepted, all over the world, as the symbol of ultimate evil' (Holocaust Forum 2000). On the one hand, the suffering of European Jews has been universalized to affirm the importance of human rights and as an admonishment to future crimes against humanity. Yet, on the other hand, the Holocaust has become a kind of negative foundation for the renewal of Europe after the Second World War.

In a larger sense, one can speak of the new field of transitional justice in Latin America, Eastern Europe and South Africa (Minow 1998). National apology, reparations and public redress have been labeled by Avishai Margalit as an 'ethics of memory' (Margalit 2002) and as a 'politics of regret' by Olick (Olick 2003: 21-32, 2007a). Each of these phrases harkens back to an important human rather than cultural trait—that of *mea culpa*. The universalization of the Holocaust as a warning about the human tendency towards barbarism is a projection of individual acknowledgment of wrongdoing onto collectives such as the nation or humanity at large (Alexander 2002). The Eichmann trial in 1961, *Holocaust* docudrama in 1979, and President von Weizsäcker's speech commemorating the 40th anniversary of the end of World War II in 1985 are but a few of the major steps towards the Holocaust becoming a cultural signifier for evil. As Helmut Dubiel writes, the Holocaust acts as a catalyst for a universal or transnational ethic. 'Today, the term "Holocaust" identifies not only the historical event, but has developed into a symbolic repertoire which has been adopted by political groups all over the world who are subjected to extreme pain and distress. It has come to denote political evil itself' (Dubiel 2003: 59). The Holocaust is a part of European history because, unlike communist crimes, the systematic killing of European Jews occurred on the continent, in both East and West Europe. As Judt writes, modern European memory shares one common reference point: that of the genocide of European Jews. 'Today the pertinent European reference is not baptism. It is extermination. Holocaust recognition is our contemporary European entry ticket' (Judt 2005: 803). Recognition of the Holocaust includes the acknowledgement of anti-Semitism as part of European tradition and culture. And it is perhaps *this* recognition that forms the basis of a common European memory. While one can speak of the Holocaust in universal terms of human evil, it was a particular element of recent European history.

The comparison of National Socialist crimes with those of communism has its intellectual origin in the West German historians' debate in the 1980s. Indeed one might argue that the contours of the debate are central to the Western narrative of World War II. The fact that the debate, which occurred in prominent West German newspapers resonated beyond academia is tantamount to its' moral and political significance. The question of how to integrate the Holocaust into German history focused on two central issues: uniqueness of the Holocaust versus comparison with crimes of communism and historicization versus normalization of the past.[2] From the numerous issues that the historians' debate opened, one issue is echoed in contemporary Eastern Europe—that of historical comparison. Can and should National Socialism be compared with communism or are they *sui generis* completely different? The question is an important one because comparison is a necessary tool for historical distinction. As Claus Leggewie put it, comparison raises the question of whether Nazism and communism are 'equally criminal' both as ideologies and as historically existing regimes (Leggewie 2006). The fact that the historians' debate was a western discussion doesn't preclude future debates in Eastern Europe. As Judt remarked, 'The war and especially the post-war years are still largely unexplored territory in the historiography of this region (in any language), and Leszek Kolakowski is doubtless correct when he predicts that eastern Europe is in for a painful *Historikerstreit* of its own'(Judt 2002: 180).

Since 1989 two parallel discourses can be heard by European political elites and intellectuals: the Holocaust as foundational symbol of a new Europe devoted to human rights and a subsequent plea by many East Europeans to recognize the crimes of communism into a common European memory. If the first discourse relies on the uniqueness of the Holocaust, the second demands a rethinking of totalitarianism. In 2004, the European Peoples Party and European Democrats Group in the European Parliament adopted a resolution condemning totalitarian communism. In April 2008, they again and unsuccessfully called for a common EU stance on communist crimes (EPP-ED 2008). They met with success in April 2009 when the European Parliament passed a Resolution on European Conscience and Totalitarianism (European Parliament Resolution 2009). Although the resolution acknowledges the suffering of those under totalitarian regimes in Europe, it carefully maintains the uniqueness of the Holocaust. The Resolution also calls for August 23 (the anniversary of the Molotov-Ribbentrop Pact) as a Europe-wide Day of Remembrance for the victims of totalitarian and authoritarian regimes. The resolution thus reflects the views of both new and old European member states. If new Europeans tend to emphasize the similarities of communism and Nazism as totalitarian regimes, old Europeans maintain the uniqueness of the Holocaust.

Are the crimes of the Gulag deemed less important because we don't have pictures to direct public attention and remind us of what happened? There is, as Susan Sontag notes a 'perpetual recirculation' of Holocaust imagery in textbooks, documentary programs and museum exhibitions (Sontag 2003: 87). Indeed the recent proliferation of Holocaust museums, first in Yad Vashem, then Washington DC and the Jewish Museum in Berlin testifies not only to the enormity

---

2 See *Historikerstreit: Die Dokumentation der Kontroverse um die Einzigartigkeit der nationalsozialistischen Judenvernichtung*, Piper 1987, *Forever in the Shadow of Hitler? The Dispute about the German Understanding of History*, trans. James Knowlton and Truett Cates, Highlands: Humanities Press, 1993. Also Charles S. Maier *The Unmasterable Past: History, Holocaust and German National Identity*. Cambridge, MA: Harvard University Press, 1988. Dan Diner, ed., *Ist der Nationalsozialismus Geschichte? Zu Historisierung und Historikerstreit*. Fischer, 1987.

of the crimes, but to a certain desire to make sure that the crimes are not forgotten and repeated. In the Baltics, the memory of national suffering under Soviet and Nazi occupation tends to occlude the centrality of the Holocaust. In the 1990s three new history museums were built in each of the Baltic States: the Estonian Occupation Museum in Tallinn, the Documentation Centre for Totalitarianism in Riga and Museum of Genocide Victims in Vilnius (Wulf 2007).

American historian Charles Maier argues that one can distinguish between the memories of Holocaust and the Gulag using the metaphor of radioactivity. Maier is not arguing about which experience was worse, 'but about which has remained engraved in memory – historical, personal – more indelibly' (Maier 2002). Like Appelbaum and others, he asks why the moral outrage surrounding the Holocaust is stronger than that of the Gulag. 'The Communist past has been remarkably *unburdensome*; (*sic*) it lingers with an incredible lightness of being' (Maier 2002). The Holocaust is hot because the sense of shame is so prevalent. Interestingly enough, the communist legacy doesn't seem to promote such soul-searching. Indeed in contemporary Russia, Stalin is widely regarded as one of the greatest Russian leaders (Gudkov 2005).

The Resolution on European Conscience and Totalitarianism is important because it can begin to address three difficulties. First of all, by calling for greater openness of archives, messy and uneven levels of occupation and collaboration in the different countries can be examined. The work of historical commissions in the various countries is important in establishing what happened during the war and communist period.[3] Trials of high-profile individuals involved in political crimes are important for understanding the complexity of the recent past. Secondly, the legacy of the West European Left has blocked a common European definition of communism. For many in the West European Left, communism is both a viable ideology and political party within European parliamentary democracy. The West European Left has a completely different understanding of communism from the East European lived experience of state-socialism. Thirdly, the difficulty in

---

3   Partially in response to international criticism about the lack of knowledge of war crimes and in an earnest attempt to document recent history, each of the Baltic States established historical commissions in the 1990s to investigate the Nazi and communist occupations. The work of these commissions is ongoing and may provide a forthright historical analysis of the war and communist regimes in the different countries. Focusing on three time periods, the first Soviet occupation 1940-1941, the Nazi occupation, 1941-1944 and the second Soviet occupation 1944-1991, the work of the Estonian History Commission is published in English only, with summaries in Estonian and Russian (Hiio 2006). Because the report of the Estonian Commission is academic, lengthy and not fully available in Estonian or Russian, it has unsurprisingly inspired little public debate. Indeed few Estonians are probably even aware of the detailed work of the commission (Onken 2007b, Hackmann 2008). To date, the Estonian Commission has published its findings in a lengthy book documenting the years 1940-1945 (*Estonia 1940-1945*). In February 2008, the creation of a Memory Institute was announced by President Toomas Hendrik Ilves to continue the investigations from 1944 to 1991 (Foundation 2008).

comparing the Holocaust with the Gulag raises the question of whether Europe needs a single common memory to hold it together or whether a plurality of memories can simultaneously and respectfully co-exist? This is a very tall order given the variety of historical experiences within the continent. I believe that one should preserve the historical specificity of the Holocaust while simultaneously recognizing the crimes of communism. Such recognition involves a rethinking of the values of pluralism and empathy that form the core of modern liberal democracy.

Pluralism, Empathy and Agreeing to Disagree

Since 1989, with the re-emergence of nation-states formerly occupied by the Soviet Union, it is not surprising that cultural conceptions of national identity and *Volkgeist* are passionately raised (Finkielkraut 1995). Likewise the recent expansion of the EU emphasizing common European values appeals more to the Enlightenment heritage of reason and humanity. Contemporary disputes about recent history have their roots in the tenuous, often fragile relation between reason and culture—between a Kantian understanding of the Enlightenment and a Romantic plea for the primacy of culture. Is there a way to respect the distinctions of the recent past without revisionism and whitewashing? Can one respect national differences without falling into the trap of relativism? It is at this juncture that the ideas of Isaiah Berlin and Hannah Arendt offer a way out of the straitjacket of monism and grand narratives.

In his clear prosaic style, Berlin argues against the impulse to explain everything according to one simple theory. While the hedgehog knows one thing very well, it is the fox, who knows many even contradictory things. The long tradition of monism, of discovering one truth to explain human nature and experience has historically proven dangerous. Berlin embraces an idea of the pluralism of values based upon different cultures. 'The enemy of pluralism is monism – the ancient belief that there is a single harmony of truths into which everything, if it is genuine, in the end must fit' (Berlin 1998: 14). Pluralism means that some truths will conflict with one another and that not all understandings can fit together into a single narrative. In various essays, Berlin reflects on the Romantic roots of pluralism that can be found in the thinking of Vico and Herder. In the 18th century, Vico emphasized that each culture has its own understanding of truth. Likewise with Herder, each culture contains the center of gravity within itself. These Romantic insights are critical for liberal pluralism because we cannot be tolerant of others without a certain degree of respect for cultural difference.

> If pluralism is a valid view, and respect between systems of values which are not necessarily hostile to each other is possible, then toleration and liberal consequences follow, as they do not either from monism (only one set of values is true, all the others are false) or from relativism (my values are mine, yours are

yours, and if we clash, too bad, neither of us can claim to be right). My political pluralism is a product of reading Vico and Herder, and of understanding the roots of romanticism, which in its violent pathological form went too far for human toleration. (Berlin 1998: 13)

Berlin is wisely cautious about making a virtue out of necessity. While each culture is unique, he does not go so far as to argue that each culture is closed to foreigners and that we can never find common grounds of understanding. His pluralism is not relativism.

I came to the conclusion that there is a plurality of ideals, as there is a plurality of cultures and of temperaments. I am not a relativist; I do not say 'I like my coffee with milk and you like it without; I am in favour of kindness and you prefer concentration camps' – each of us has our own values, which cannot be overcome or integrated. This I believe to be false. But I do believe that there is a plurality of values which men can and do seek, and that these values differ. (Berlin 1998: 11)

With Berlin, the door is open to toleration and empathy. In short, living in a democracy means that individuals can agree to disagree. Consensus isn't possible on all issues, particularly on ones that are based upon history or culture. The best we can hope for is respectful disagreement. Agreeing to disagree means that small narratives are an intrinsic part of democracy. A general framework of respect for pluralism as a value in itself leads to toleration and the ability to live with many different truths without recourse to violence to preserve one's cultural identity. 'Members of one culture can, by the force of imaginative insight, understand (what Vico called *entrare*) the values, the ideals, the forms of life of another culture or society, even those remote in time and space' (Berlin 2003: 10).

Because pluralism takes seriously the fact that cultural differences matter, certain truths and understandings potentially overlap. Pluralism draws from the rich tradition of both the Enlightenment and Romanticism. 'That is why pluralism is not relativism—the multiple values are objective, part of the essence of humanity rather than arbitrary creations of men's subjective fancies' (Berlin 1998: 12). Pluralism is linked to a deep appreciation of humanity. At the end of the day, it is our humanity that human beings have in common. It is at this juncture that Berlin complements the hermeneutic tradition of Gadamer. Tradition and history inevitably influence the perspective of individuals; likewise there exist a multitude of truths. 'Intercommunication between cultures in time and space is only possible because what makes men human is common to them, and acts as a bridge between them' (Berlin 2003: 11).

Hannah Arendt's discussion of plurality is rooted in her argument that totalitarianism as a new political phenomenon of the twentieth century explodes traditional modes of understanding. Crystallizing the elements of mass terror, anti-Semitism, imperialism and ideology, totalitarianism attempts to destroy all aspects of the individual. The political achievements of the Enlightenment embodied in the dignity of man and man as a rights-bearing citizen were rendered meaningless with the totalitarian movements of National Socialism and Stalinist communism.

> Total domination, which strives to organize the infinity plurality and differentiation of human beings as if all of humanity were just one individual, is possible only if each and every person can be reduced to a never-changing identity of reactions, so that each of these bundles of reactions can be exchanged at random for any other. (Arendt 1973: 438)

Total domination occurs in three phases. Firstly, the juridical concept of the person is destroyed removing individuals from the protection of the law. Secondly, the moral concept of the person is destroyed by removing possibilities for moral choice of action due to fear and mistrust. Finally, total domination results in the destruction of the uniqueness of the individual symbolized in the bureaucratic administration of the concentration camp. 'The concentration and extermination camps of totalitarian regimes serve as the laboratories in which the fundamental belief of totalitarianism that everything is possible is being verified' (Arendt 1973: 437).

Throughout her writings, Arendt highlights the theme of plurality. Similar to Berlin, she is wary of forcing the complexity of political life into one theory. Just as Kant articulated that each individual is an end in himself and can never be rationalized as a means towards an ideological goal or political end, so Arendt also argues for a conception of the person as one who has the rights to have rights, as one who commands respect from others simply on the basis of their sheer humanity. Freedom is not about the freedom to think alone; one always thinks in the company of others. A concept of the person as an end in him or herself entails dignity, respect and an ability to think from the perspective of the other person. It entails a possibility for empathy and understanding with others. The Arendtian polis is constructed out of the words and actions of equal individuals who reveal their distinctiveness to one another through public debate.

> Human plurality, the basic condition of both action and speech, has the twofold character of equality and distinction. If men were not equal, they could neither understand each other and those who came before them nor plan for the future and foresee the needs of who will come after them. If men were not distinct, each human being distinguished from any other who is, was, or will be, they would need neither speech nor action to make themselves understood. (Arendt 1958: 175-176)

Distinction is an equal differentiation, a recognition of difference, or uniqueness; not a hierarchical categorization. Difference suggests plurality because plurality reveals a variety of equals possessing different opinions. Arendt does not conceive of difference as a hierarchical classification for the sake of excluding unwanted members from the polis. 'Human plurality is the paradoxical plurality of unique being' (Arendt 1958: 176). She does not explicitly view difference as a tool for exclusion, but rather as a positive and indeed necessary element for political discourse. 'Plurality is the condition of human action because we are all the same, that is, human, in such a way that nobody is ever the same as anyone else who ever lived, lives, or will live' (Arendt 1958: 8). The human condition of action is plurality, or a life lived among human beings, and the human condition of work is worldliness—whereby individuals construct a common world in which freedom and equality can appear. The polis is not natural, but man-made and public. For Arendt, 'we are not born equal, we become equal as members of a group' (Arendt 1973: 301). Thus, we might say that the private world is the world in which we are naturally born unequal; however we experience a second birth when we are born into the polis, into the communal clearing where equality and freedom can appear.

Each person represents a new beginning, a new and unique individual possessing the potential for action and speech. Each newcomer must answer the question 'who are you?' (Arendt 1958: 10) And each time we are asked this question we have the possibility through speech and action to create a new beginning or a new story. Each individual is unique. 'With the creation of man, the principle of beginning came into the world itself, which, of course, is only another way of saying that the principle of freedom was created when man was created but not before' (Arendt 1958: 177). Just as St. Augustine located the will in the fact that each person is a beginner, so Arendt finds that our will to do something, to become something, is linked to our creativity and plurality. Likewise Arendt invoked the change of Saul into Paul as a metaphor for human beginning and the capacity for change. One is not doomed to a predestined life, but has the possibility to change, learn from our mistakes and to begin again.

Concluding Remarks

The different interpretations of World War II in Europe since 1989 reveal three broad narratives: Western, Soviet/Russian, and post-communist/post-Soviet. Each narrative emphasizes different experiences of the war and subsequent Cold War epoch. Recent requests from East European countries for EU-wide recognition of the crimes of communism are important because different interpretations of the past are discussed publicly. Since pluralism is a value in itself within Europe—East and West Europeans can agree to disagree on whether the crimes of communism can be compared with the crimes of National Socialism or not. The fact that in Estonia, national suffering tends to occlude the centrality of the Holocaust does not preclude closer understanding and empathy in the future. The case is different though with respect to the Russian Federation and the Baltic States. Until the Russian Federation, as the successor state to the Soviet Union acknowledges publicly the crimes of communism, one cannot expect respectful disagreement between the countries. To the contrary, recent debates over monuments and commemorative holidays have demonstrated sharp differences between Russia and the Baltic States. If the Baltic States (Estonia in particular) view the role of the USSR as both a liberator and occupier of Eastern Europe, Russian officials remember the role of the Red Army as the heroic liberator of Europe from fascism.

Pluralism entails respect for different memories of the past and recognition of difference. If the legacy of the past is merely used as a tool for short-term political gain, the possibility of learning about the past for the sake of future is lost. The pluralism of Isaiah Berlin and Hannah Arendt offers a way to move beyond the settling of scores in the past towards a respectful understanding of historical difference. If there is a lesson to be learned from the legacies of recent history, it is that disrespect and resentment only fuel stereotypes and misunderstanding. Agreeing to disagree is neither a whitewashing of the past nor a grand narrative, but an acknowledgement of different conflicting memories of historical events.

References

Adorno, T. 1986. What does Coming to Terms with the Past Mean?, trans. Geoffrey Hartman. *Bitburg in Moral and Political Perspective.* Bloomington, IN: Indiana University Press.
Alexander, J. 2002. On the Social Construction of Moral Universals. *European Journal of Social Theory*, 5:1, 5-85.
Alexander, J. et al. 2004. *Cultural Trauma and Collective Identity*. Berkeley, CA: University of California Press.
Anderson, B. 1991 (1983). *Imagined Communities: Reflections on the Origin and Spread of Nationalism.* London: Verso.
Appelbaum, A. 2003. *Gulag: A History.* New York: Penguin Books.
Arendt, H. 1958. *The Human Condition.* Chicago, IL: University of Chicago.
Arendt, H. 1973. *The Origins of Totalitarianism.* San Diego: Harcourt Brace Jovanovich.
Ash, T.G. 2002. Trials, Purges and History Lessons: Treating a Difficult Past in Post-communist Europe, in *Memory and Power in Postwar Europe: Studies in the Presence of the Past.* Cambridge: Cambridge University Press. 265-282.
Assmann, J. 1995. Collective Memory and Cultural Identity, trans. John Czaplicka. *New German Critique*, no. 65, Spring-Summer, 125-133.
Assmann, A. 2006. *Der lange Schatten der Vergangenheit: Erinnerungskultur und Geschichtspolitik.* Munich: C.H. Beck.
Barnouw, D. 2005. *The War in the Empty Air: Victims, Perpetrators, and Postwar Germans.* Bloomington, IN: Indiana University Press.
Bauman, Z. 1989. *Modernity and the Holocaust.* Ithaca, NY: Cornell University Press.
Beevor, A. 2002. *Berlin: The Downfall 1945.* London: Penguin Books.

Bell, D. ed. 2006. *Memory, Trauma and World Politics: Reflections on the Relations between Past and Present.* London: Palgrave Macmillan.

Benjamin, W. 1968. Theses on the Philosophy of History, in *Illuminations*, trans. Harry Zohn. New York: Schocken Books.

Berlin, I. 1998. My Intellectual Path in *The Power of Ideas.* Princeton, NJ: Princeton University Press, 1-23.

Berlin, I. 2003. The Pursuit of the Ideal, in *The Crooked Timber of Humanity: Chapters in the History of Ideas.* London: Pimlico, 1-19.

Bude, H. 1992. *Bilanz der Nachfolge.* Frankfurt: Suhrkamp.

Burke, P. 2004. *What is Cultural History?* Cambridge: Polity Press.

Challand, B. 2009 (1989), Contested Memories and the Shifting Cognitive Maps of Europe. *European Journal of Social Theory*, 12:3, August, 397-408.

Confino, A. 2006. Collective Memory and Cultural History: Problems of Method in *Germany as a Culture of Remembrance: Promises and Limits of Writing History.* Chapel Hill: University of North Carolina Press.

Connerton, P. 1989. *How Societies Remember*. New York: Cambridge University Press.

Cooper, B., ed. 1999. *War Crimes: The Legacy of Nuremberg*. New York: TV Books.

Davies, N. 2006. *Europe at War. 1939-1945: No Simple Victory*. London: Pan Books.

Diner, D. ed. 1987. *Ist der Nationalsozialismus Geschichte? Zu Historisierung und Historikerstreit.* Frankfurt am Main: Fischer.

Diner, D. 2003. Restitution and Memory: The Holocaust in European Political Cultures. *New German Critique*. Fall, 90, 36-44.

Dubiel, H. 2003. The Remembrance of the Holocaust as a Catalyst for a Transnational Ethic? *New German Critique*, Fall, 90, 59-70.

EPP-ED. Group in the European Parliament. Resolution adopted by the XVIth EEP Congress Condemning totalitarian Communism. February 4-5, 2004. Available at http://www.epp-ed.eu/Press/peve04/eve01/res-communism_en.asp? Accessed April 26, 2008.

Estonia 1940-1945. Available at www.historycommission.ee.

European Parliament Resolution on European Conscience and Totalitarianism. 2009. Available at http://www.europarl.europa.eu/pdfs/news/expert/infopress/20090401IPR53245/20090401IPR53245_en.pdf. Accessed April 3, 2009.

Finkielkraut, A. 1995. *The Defeat of the Mind*, trans. Judith Friedlander. New York: Columbia University Press.

Forever in the Shadow of Hitler? The Dispute about the German Understanding of History. 1993, trans. James Knowlton and Truett Cates. Highlands: Humanities Press.

Foundation. 2008. Foundation for the Investigation of the Communist Crimes. Estonia to Probe Soviet-era Abuses. February 1, 2008. Available at http://www.haaba.com/news/2008/02/01/7-84989/estonia-to-probe-sovietera-abuses.html. Accessed January 28, 2009.

Friedländer, S. 1992. *Probing the Limits of Representation: Nazism and the Final Solution.* Cambridge, MA: Harvard University Press.

Gadamer, H.G. 1975. *Truth and Method*, trans. Joel Winsheimer and Donald G. Marshall. New York: Crosswood Publishing.
Giesen, B. 2004. *Triumph and Trauma*. Boulder, CO: Paradigm Publishers.
Grass, G. 2004. *Crabwalk*. New York: Harvest Books.
Grass, G. 2007. *Peeling the Onion*. New York: Harvest Books.
Gudkov, L. 2005. The Fetters of Victory. How the War provides Russia with its Identity. *Osteuropa* 4-6. Accessed in *Eurozine*, March 13, 2007. Available at www.eurozine.xom/articles/2005-05-03-gudkov-en.html, 5.
Habermas, J. 1993. On the Public Use of History: The Official Self-Understanding of the Federal Republic is Breaking Up in *Forever in the Shadow of Hitler?*, trans. James Knowlton and Truett Cates. Highlands, NJ: Humanities Press.
Habermas, J. 2001. The Postnational Constellation and the Future of Democracy in *The Postnational Constellation: Political Essays*. London: Polity Press, 58-112.
Hackmann, J. 2009. From National Victims to Transnational Bystanders? The Changing Commemoration of World War II in Central and Eastern Europe. *Constellations: An International Journal of Critical and Democratic Theory*, 16:1, March, 167-181.
Halbwachs, M. 1980 (1950). *The Collective Memory*, trans. Francis J. Ditter, Jr. and Vida Yazdi Ditter. New York: Harper Colophon.
Halbwachs, M. 1992 (1941). *On Collective Memory*, trans. Lewis A. Coser. Chicago, IL: University of Chicago Press.
Hiio, T., et al,. 2006. *Estonia 1940-1945: Reports of the Estonian International Commission for the Investigation of Crimes against Humanity.* Tallinn: Estonian Foundation for the Investigation of Crimes against Humanity.
Historikerstreit: Die Dokumentation der Kontroverse um die Einzigartigkeit der nationalsozialistischen Judenvernichtung, 1987. Munich: Piper.
Hobsbawm, E. 1983. Mass-Producing Traditions: Europe, 1870-1914 in *The Invention of Tradition*, edited by Eric Hobsbawm and Terence Ranger. Cambridge: Cambridge University Press, 263-307.
Holocaust Forum. 2000. Stockholm, January 2000. Available at www.holocaustforum.gov.se.
Jaspers, K. 1961 (1947). *The Question of German Guilt*, trans. E.B. Ashton. New York: Capricorn Books.
Judt, T. 2002. The Past is Another Country: Myth and Memory in Post-war Europe, in *Memory and Power in Post-War Europe*, edited by Jan-Werner Müller. Cambridge: Cambridge University Press, 157-183.
Judt, T. 2005. *Postwar: A History of Europe since 1945*. New York: Penguin Press.
Kõresaar, E. 2005. *Elu ideoloogiad (Life Ideologies)*. Tartu: Eesti Rahva Muuseum.
Koselleck, R. 1985. 'Space of Experience' and 'Horizon of Expectation': Two Historical Categories', in *Futures Past: On the Semantics of Historical Time*, trans. Keith Tribe. Cambridge, MA: MIT Press.
Lebow, R.N. 2006. The Memory of Politics in Postwar Europe, in *The Politics of Memory in Postwar Europe*, edited by Richard Ned Lebow, Wulf Kansteiner, Claudio Fogu. Durham, NC: Duke University Press, 1-39.

Leggewie, C. 2006. Equally Criminal? Totalitarian Experience and European Memory. Originally in *Transit*, June 2006. Available at www.eurozine.com. Accessed August 18, 2008.

Lowenthal, D. 1985. *The Past is a Foreign Country*. New York: Cambridge University Press.

Maier, C.S. 1988. *The Unmasterable Past: History, Holocaust and German National Identity*. Cambridge, MA: Harvard University Press.

Maier, C.S. 2002. Hot Memory ... Cold Memory: On the Political Half-Life of Fascist and Communist Memory. *Transit: Europäische Revue*, Number 22, Winter 2001/2002, 153-165. Available at http://www.iwm.at/index2.php?option=com_content&task=view&id=316&Itemid=481. Accessed February 24, 2008.

Mannheim, K. 1952 (1928). The Problem of Generations, in *Essays on the Sociology of Knowledge*. London: Routledge and Kegan Paul, 276-322.

Margalit. A. 2002. *The Ethics of Memory*. Cambridge, MA: Harvard University Press.

Minow, M. 1998. *Between Vengeance and Forgiveness: Facing History after Genocide and Mass Violence*. Boston, MA: Beacon Books.

Mitscherlich, A. and M. 1975. *The Inability to Mourn*, trans. Veberly R. Placzek. New York: Grove Press.

'MEPs call for EU stance on Communist Crimes.' 2008. http: EUobservor.com/9/26021?rss_rk=1 April 22, 2008. Accessed April 26, 2008.

Motyl, A. J. 2008. Warum ist die KGB-Bar möglich? *Transit*, 35: Summer, 104-122.

Nietzsche, F. 1980 (1874). *On the Advantage and Disadvantage of History for Life*, trans. Peter Preuss. Indianapolis, IN: Hackett Publishing.

Nora, P. 1989. Between Memory and History: Les Lieux de Mémoire. *Representations* 26, Spring: 7-25.

Nora, P. 1996. *Realms of Memory: The Construction of the French Past*, trans. Arthur Goldhammer. New York: Columbia University Press.

Oathwaite, W. and Ray, L. 2005. Modernity, Memory and Postcommunism in *Social Theory and Postcommunism*. London: Blackwell, 176-196.

Olick, J.K. 2003. The Value of Regret? Lessons from and for Germany, in *Justice and the Politics of Memory: Religion and Public Life*, edited by Gabriel. R. Ricci. New Brunswick, NJ: Transaction Books, 21-32.

Olick. J.K. 2007a. From Usable Pasts to the Return of the Repressed. *Hedgehog Review*, 9:2.

Olick, J.K. 2007b. *The Politics of Regret: On Collective Memory and Historical Responsibility*. New York: Routledge.

Olschowsky, B. 2008. Erinnerungslandschaft mit Brücken. *Transit*, 35, Summer, 23-49.

Onken, E.C. 2007a. The Baltic States and Moscow's 9 May Commemoration: Analysing Memory Politics in Europe. *Europe-Asia Studies*, 59:1, January.

Onken, E.C. 2007b. The Politics of Finding Historical Truth: Reviewing Baltic History Commissions and their Work. *Journal of Baltic Studies*, 38:1, 109-116.

Petersoo, P. and Tamm, M. eds. 2008. *Monumentaalne konflikt: Mälu, poliitika ja identiteet tänapäeva Eestis* (*Monumental Conflict: Memory, Politics and Identity in Contemporary Estonia*). Tallinn: Varrak.

Ricoeur, P. 1991. The Human Experience of Time and Narrative, in *A Ricoeur Reader: Reflection and Imagination.* Toronto: University of Toronto Press.

Schwan, G. 2001. *Politics and Guilt: The Destructive Power of Silence*, trans. Thomas Dunlap. Lincoln, NE: University of Nebraska.

Sebald, W.G. 2003. *On the Natural History of Destruction*, trans. Anthea Bell. New York: Random House.

Shils, E. 1981. *Tradition.* Chicago, IL: University of Chicago Press.

Snyder, T. 2010. *Bloodlands: Europe Between Hitler and Stalin.* New York: Basic Books.

Sontag, S. 2003. *Regarding the Pain of Others.* New York: Picador.

Wulf, M. 2007. The struggle for official recognition of 'displaced' group memories in post-Soviet Estonia, in *Past in the Making: Recent History Revisions and Historical Revisionism in Central Europe after 1989*, edited by Michal Kopecek. Budapest and New York: Central European Press, 217-241.

Chapter 3
The Ethics of Seeing: Photographs of Germany at the End of the War

In one of her last books, *Regarding the Pain of Others*, Susan Sontag reflects on the strangeness of the term collective memory. 'What is called collective memory is not a remembering but a stipulating: that *this* is important and this is the story about how it happened, with the pictures that lock the story in our minds' (Sontag 2003: 86). Since memory, in her opinion, is a deeply personal and individual experience, photography changes the ways in which the past can be represented and remembered. The invention of photography transforms a private experience into something public and shared. Sontag is concerned with the iconic status of photographs to represent one story of the past as *the* only story. During the process from individual to collective image, documentary photographs become 'the visual equivalent of sound bites' (Ibid.). Images, like sound bites tend to flatten out details in favor of something that shocks and draws attention. Photographs do indeed capture important aspects of the past; however they also project a kind of authoritative concreteness and unity. If an image becomes iconic, it risks hiding the complexity of historical events into a frozen moment. Sontag's rejection of the term 'collective memory' is more than a semantic parsing of words. Rather, it is related to the enormous power that images have to shape not only what is remembered from the past but; how the complexity of historical events is remembered and narrated. She is concerned with the ideological power that images inherently possess. The fact that Sontag has written not only one, but two books on the power of representation, highlighting photography in particular—without including even one image in those books testifies to the power that she ascribes to the image. 'Photographs objectify: they turn an event or a person into something that can be possessed. And photographs are a species of alchemy, for all that they are prized as a transparent account of reality' (Ibid., 81). Photographs possess a magical ability to attract, frame, narrate and sear an event into our minds.

We live in a visual culture, a culture of the image and of the copy. Photography has indelibly changed the way in which we experience the present and think about the recent past. Because World War II was the first event that photojournalists documented in such detail, its images are important not only for an understanding of what happened, but also for a phenomenological study of how we perceive what happened. There have been numerous accounts and debates about how the Holocaust defied human imagination and reached the limits of representation. Saul Friedlander's poetic discussion of how images of

Jew and Nazi provide stereotypical images of good and evil while reducing the complexity of the Third Reich to clichés has a profound resonance in subsequent mediations of how World War II and the Holocaust are represented. Likewise, James Young's poignant mediations on the controversy surrounding artistic monuments to the Holocaust suggest the enormous power of representation and image (Friedländer 1992, Young 1993).

In two different books, Dagmar Barnouw and Barbie Zelizer analyze ways in which documentary photographs of Germany at the end of the war have contributed to how history is narrated and remembered. Both Barnouw's book *Germany 1945: Views of War and Violence* and Zelizer's, *Remembering to Forget: Holocaust Memory through the Camera's Eye* analyze images from World War II taken by documentary photographers and Allied army photographers. Their subject matter, however, is different. Barnouw focuses on how photographs taken by Allied photojournalists and army officers deliberately sought (and found) a defiant and numbed German nation; while Zelizer examines photographs taken at the liberation of the concentration camps on the western front. One is a study primarily of 'the Germans' and the other of 'the Jews.' As such, the books complement one another very well. Each presents troubling and moving images of human suffering on an unprecedented scale. Both authors also echo Sontag's melancholic and poetic reflections on the modern invention of photography.

Photography provides us, as Sontag wrote in *On Photography*, with a grammar and 'ethics of seeing.' 'In teaching us a new visual code, photographs alter and enlarge our notions of what is worth looking at and what we have a right to observe. They are a grammar and, even more importantly, an ethics of seeing' (Sontag 1990: 3). From Plato onwards, ours is a dualistic world, of contrast between image and reality, darkness and light. Sontag reflects on various ways that photography has changed everyday experience and our perception of historical events. How can seeing have anything to do with ethics? Why would photography, as a new form of making pictures have any kind of ethical consequences? Here, Sontag is unparalleled in her observations. 'Humankind lingers unregeneratively in Plato's cave, still reveling, its age-old habit, in mere images of the truth…This very insatiability of the photographing eye changes the terms of the confinement in the cave, our world' (Ibid., 3). She draws attention to how photography and the ability to mechanically reproduce pictures change the terms of our life in the cave and world of appearance. The dualism between appearance and reality, inside and outside still remains; what changes are 'the terms of confinement.' Photography provides the illusion of closeness and distance. When we see a picture, we are brought closer to the people in the picture. We can 'see' the humanity of that person. Yet, at the same time, photographs can distance us from the reality of an event. The frame of an image already separates it from the everyday flow of time. Likewise, photography is Janus-faced in that it can both support and undermine political power. Photography can both empower the state with unprecedented tools of propaganda *and* promote democratization by making everyone their own historian.

Photography provides the illusion of evidence, of the objective facts of an event. Due to this demonstrative power, photography possesses a truth telling aspect that traditional art does not. But because photographs validate historical events, they contain the potential to become *the* authoritative representation of the past. As Sontag notes, photographs both capture and create reality, and therein lie their allure. 'Photographs furnish evidence ... The picture may distort; but there is always a presumption that something exists, or did exist, which is like what's in the picture' (Ibid., 5). Documenting the crime scene, furnishing evidence that something happened is a vitally important aspect of photography. Yet, in reflecting on photojournalism, Sontag notes how the task of the photojournalist is not to intervene, but to record. 'Photographing is essentially an act of non-intervention.' Granted, one might argue that famous pictures have aroused emotion and public outcry against atrocity and war. Her point though is well taken because the desire to capture the perfect image may cloud one's capacity to act. Seeing has moral consequences for both the photographer and the viewer. In times of war, as well as social and political upheaval, photography has the power to frame an event and suggest how a picture *should* be understood. 'Photographs cannot create a moral position, but they can reinforce one – and can help build a nascent one' (Ibid., 17). Both Zelizer and Barnouw examine how photographs of Germany from the perspective of civilians and concentration camp victims reinforced a moral position about the German nation and the German people at the end of the war. Some photographs, such as those of concentration camp victims have become 'ethical reference points' or markers on a map portraying the kind of crimes human beings are capable of committing in the name of a political ideal (Ibid., 21).

Germany 1945

In *Germany 1945: Views of War and Violence*, Dagmar Barnouw makes the strong argument that documentary photojournalists did not simply capture the past but rather helped to create a moral position of self-righteousness still prevalent today. For her, such a moral position represents a one-dimensional picture of historical reality. After her introduction, in which she pleads for the necessity to re-examine photos from the end of the war, *Germany 1945* is divided into chapters comparing Allied photojournalism with documentary photographs taken by German photographers. Barnouw demonstrates how German photographers were especially sensitive to the plight of German civilians and POWs and thereby avoided the assumption of collective guilt that the Allied and especially American photographers assumed in 1945 and shortly thereafter. She was 'interested not so much in revisiting the meanings of that "German catastrophe" as in looking at *expectations* (*sic*) about how Germans as a group could or should cope with it' (Barnouw 1996: ix). For her, the German question is not about belated nationhood, regression to barbarism, intentional or functional arguments for National Socialism—but a question of perception and representation. Because Germany lost the war, it is of crucial importance that the dominant pictures were taken by the victors, liberators, outsiders, and non-Germans looking at Germans. Barnouw is interested in the expectation of those photographers, in what they expected to find, what they discovered, and what they actually found. For the expectation already prejudiced the photographic eye. They did not simply capture reality 'as it was' but also created it.

In aptly-titled chapters, Barnouw unsettles some of the certainties of how Germany in 1945 was captured on film and remembered for posterity. The first chapter, entitled 'To Make Them See,' examines how the images taken by Allied photographers, the de-Nazification program, and the decisions to have German civilians bury concentration camp dead all were meant to make Germans see what happened during the Third Reich. In particular, she emphasizes the importance of documentary photographs in the Allied effort to make ordinary Germans 'see' what was done in their name. De-Nazification measures ordered Germans to undergo a democratic rebirth complete with a totally changed perspective on past experiences. Germans, who were forced to fill out the notorious questionnaires about their activities and affiliations during the Nazi period, had to accept a past constructed from the hindsight of the Holocaust—a past, in which, as often as not, they might not recognize themselves (Ibid., 5).

U.S. Army Signal Corps photography units documented German civilians' confrontation with German atrocities. As such, many of their photographs are about Germans looking at mass graves, reburying the dead—all under the watchful eyes of American or British soldiers. Moreover, Barnouw notes the overwhelming presence of women and children who were 'made to see.' Here she raises questions about why children were taken to these mass graves and made to see what was done in their name. The photographs are important 'witnesses' to the past. In painstaking detail, Barnouw demonstrates that the photographs were not only captured as evidence but also taken with the moral message of indignation and disbelief. Chapter 2, 'The Quality of Victory and the "German Question,"' carefully analyzes the dramatic implications that *Life* magazine photojournalism had for the presumption of German collective guilt and the expectation of finding a defiant demoralized nation. In this chapter—as well as the following chapter, 'What They Saw'—Barnouw stresses the one-dimensional character of these images. Many of the photographs that were published in *Life* magazine, under such issue titles as 'The German Atrocities' and 'The German People,' have become cultural icons— 'icons of cultural failure and we have been forced or forced ourselves, to looks at them again and again' (Ibid., 79). In particular, Barnouw takes issue with the stark pictures of Margaret Bourke-White in her book, *Dear Fatherland, Rest Quietly*. For her, Bourke-White was uninterested in the complexity of the immediate postwar situation for German civilians. German and British photographers were less prejudiced and more open to document the ambiguity and horror of the German defeat. She contrasts American photographs of German civilians looking at corpses with photographs by *Life* magazine of displaced German civilians. Barnouw carefully outlines the contempt many photojournalists (especially Bourke-White) seemed to express for German suffering.

> These displaced Germans are being treated callously but not with the deliberate cruelty which their government once inflicted on others. They are, at least, allowed to live. These people allowed themselves (*sic*) to fall so low in the eyes of the world that the world, seeing their suffering, find it hard to feel sorry for them. (Ibid., 102)

According to Barnouw, German photojournalists did not seem to pass judgment on their subjects. In her penultimate chapter, 'Words and Images,' she discusses German photojournalism and responses by German exiles to Germany in 1945. It is here that she substantiates her claim that many Allied photojournalists helped to create a singular image of German collective guilt, whereas German photographers conveyed the complexity of Germans living during the Third Reich. Discussing the reactions of Hans Speier and Karl Jaspers, she notes how these men also came to pass judgment on Germans. In contrast, German photographs from 1945 possessed a certain grim naïveté. 'Looking and recording, most of these photographers did not respond to their expectation that their perspective be informed by the "German question" ... This is the value of these images for the later viewer: they call attention to what was there to be seen' (Ibid., 194). These evocative images of displaced civilians, destroyed families, and lost POWs are important for a fuller picture of Germany in 1945. Barnouw calls attention to how photographs shape cultural memory. Throughout the book, she questions how Germans in 1945 could have demonstrated adequate remorse, sorrow, or guilt. 'Signal Corp photographs of confrontation explicitly documented American expectations that Germans individually identify with the victims and collectively acknowledge their identity as victimizers. But, intentionally or unintentionally, they also captured the self-righteous, sometimes cruel innocence of such expectations' (Ibid., 22). *Germany 1945* is an attempt to uncover some of the prejudices and mentalities of photographs taken in 1945. As such, it complements W.G. Sebald's moving essay, 'Air War and Literature' chronicling the bombing of German cities (Sebald 2004: 3-104). Barnouw, like Sebald reflects on the complexity of Germany from the point of view of civilians who lived through the war. Likewise, without lessening the crimes of the Holocaust, her attention to civilian suffering throughout the war emphasizes how photography establishes a moral grammar and ethics of seeing.

Remembering to Forget

Allied photographs of the liberation of concentration camps have indelibly shaped historical memory of Nazi aggression and genocide. *Remembering to Forget: Holocaust Memory through the Camera's Eye* is a somber meditation on how memory also involves a certain degree of forgetfulness. Barbie Zelizer's metaphoric title suggests ways in which we have been numbed by the plethora of Holocaust imagery. Sontag also comes to mind here: 'images anesthetize, images transfix' (Sontag 1990: 20). Although photography has the potential to make the past more real and imaginable, the repetition of seeing the same images destroys their shock value. Unlike Barnouw, Zelizer primarily concentrates on photographs taken of the Allied liberation of concentration camps. After an analysis of the historical context in which many of those photographs were taken, she traces the history of concentration camp images as symbols of mass atrocity. Influenced by Halbwachs, Zelizer raises the important question of how Holocaust memory changes with the contemporary needs of society. 'Collectively held images thus act as signposts, directing people who remember to preferred meanings by the fastest route' (Zelizer 1998: 7).

Like Barnouw, Zelizer is interested in how photographs furnish authoritative evidence to the past. As tools for journalism, photographs have historically played a secondary role to a news story; however, with World War II photojournalism, the image became more important than the story. Words proved incapable of describing photographic evidence. Thus, 'an analysis of atrocity photos becomes not just a graphing of what was seen, but a consideration of how and why, and in what ways it has been remembered' (Ibid., 10). By looking at the way in which Holocaust images have been subject to 'strategic recycling' (Ibid., 12), Zelizer argues that such images not only help the viewer to remember the Holocaust as a historical event, but become frames of reference for subsequent atrocities, such as Rwanda and Bosnia. There is a danger to remember the Holocaust in stereotypical format while neglecting contemporary atrocity. Thus, the question is raised, 'how have these earlier images changed the way in which we "see" each new instance of politically sanctioned death and slaughter?' (Ibid., 13) Invoking the words of Leon Wieseltier, Zelizer cautions against looking at Holocaust photographs as pure symbols divorced from their particular historical context.

> In the contemplation of the death camps, we must be strangers; and if we are not strangers, if the names of the killers and the places of the killing and the numbers of the killed fall easily from our tongues, then we are not remembering to remember, but remembering to forget. (Wieseltier quoted in Ibid., 13)

She points out that western media reacted cautiously and skeptically to the magnitude of violence, because it was the Soviet Army that liberated the first concentration camp. When foreign correspondents were invited to Majdanek in September 1944, their reactions were minimized due to the lack of certainty. Majdanek became 'a standard for bearing witness' (Ibid., 53), a standard for how Allied photographers would frame and report the liberation of camps along the Western Front: Dachau, Bergen-Belsen, and Buchenwald. The Majdanek photographs revealed objects: gas chambers, crematoria, shoes, warehouses—but not the victims—the mounds of corpses that would appear with the Allied images of liberated camps. Once President Eisenhower demanded the coverage of Nazi atrocities, photographers and journalists flooded the western camps. Bourke-White reflected on her 'self-imposed stupor' while documenting Buchenwald (Ibid., 88). Thus, photographs symbolized truth, evidence, and above all, moral certainty.

In a chapter filled with gruesome images, 'Covering Atrocity in Image,' Zelizer recounts the rise of photojournalism in the liberation of concentration camps. Harrowing pictures of corpses, skeletal victims, and mass graves—some that will be familiar to most readers, others not—accompany her careful analysis. Like Barnouw, she demonstrates how German civilians were depicted as witnesses looking at the victims of Nazi aggression. She is most forceful when she illustrates how atrocity photographs have become symbols or cultural icons (Ibid., 108). Images were published repeatedly; many chronicling the same or similar images. 'The photos functioned not only referentially but as symbolic markers of atrocity in its broadest form' (Ibid., 111). Zelizer argues that the repetition of photographs-of mass graves, of survivors looking at the camera, of confrontation shots between survivors and guards—created a stock of generalized images: 'a commandant, a mass burial, a common grave, a charred body, human cordwool' (Ibid., 121). As the photos became more important than the captions, the specific details receded into the background. Thus, 'the exact details of the atrocities mattered less than the response of bearing witness' (Ibid., 126).

In the second half of *Remembering to Forget*, Zelizer develops her most interesting thesis—namely, how the meaning of Holocaust memory changes with the needs of society. Using the metaphor of waves, she argues for its ebb and flow. In the first wave, 'forgetting to remember,' important specific details were forgotten (names, places, actual activities of survivors) in the creation of symbolic stock images. Details were forgotten or downplayed so that the event, later named the 'Holocaust,' could be remembered. The first memory wave bore witness; in the second, amnesia set in from the late 1940s until the 1970s. By the late 1970s, things reversed as Holocaust imagery captured the public imagination. The third memory wave, 'remembering to remember,' occurred from 1970s until today. This renewed interest in Holocaust imagery exploded in the mass media with films, museums, monuments, and commemorations. However, Zelizer and others caution that these images and their continual recycling may have reached a saturation point. 'In empowering both those who seek authentication of Nazi atrocities and those who deny them, atrocity photos thereby threaten to become a representation without substance' (Ibid., 201). Because Nazi concentration camp photos were the first document of mass atrocity, they have become the standard against which subsequent atrocity is measured. Pictures of Cambodia, Rwanda, and Bosnia inevitably refer back to the European killing fields.

* * *

Both Zelizer and Barnouw are concerned with how images take on lives of their own. Both also raise the moral question of how one *should* respond to images of war and violence. The photographs of Germany at the end of the war—of concentration camps, civilians, returning POWS and soldiers offer evidence of historical fact. But they also offer testimony that seeing is not only believing or a sign of truth; 'seeing' is also subject to ideological, political and cultural trends. As Sontag cautioned in *Regarding the Pain of Others*, photographs alone are not sufficient for understanding the past. 'The problem is not that people remember through photographs, but that they remember only the photographs' (Sontag 2003: 89). Isolated images are not enough, one has to think and reflect on the meaning of those photographs. If images become sacred icons, they are lifted outside of ordinary time and no longer touch us. The point is not that we should turn away from graven images, but rather think more carefully about what we see. Sontag is interested in the moral consequences of what we do *when* and *after* we see. 'Perhaps too much value is assigned to memory, not enough to thinking. Remembering *is* an ethical act, has ethical value in and of itself' (Ibid., 115). She is interested in the lessons that can be learned from the past – in what she calls, 'collective instruction' (Ibid., 85).

> Photographs that everyone recognizes are now a constituent part of what a society chooses to think about, or declare that it has chosen to think about. It calls these ideas "memories," and that is, over the long run, a fiction. Strictly speaking, there is no such thing as collective memory – part of the same family of spurious notions as collective guilt. But there is collective instruction. (Sontag 2003: 85)

The pictures in *Germany 1945* and *Remembering to Forget* portray different aspects of Germany at the end of the war. They cannot give a complete overview or 'picture' of the past, only fragments of it. Barnouw's sympathetic reading of the moral implications of photographs of German civilians is balanced by Zelizer's harrowing argument for how images from concentration camps shocked viewers into numbed silence. As alchemy, photographs can shock and numb the viewer. It is, however, narrative that can call attention to the particular context and moral dilemmas that individuals faced in Germany during the war. Both Barnouw and Zelizer attest to Sontag's plea for the necessity of *both* narrative and image. Photography has the iconic power to capture an event and momentarily freeze time. However, in that suspension of time, one risks losing sight of the larger historical context. As Sontag ruefully notes: 'Narratives can make us understand. Photographs do something else: they haunt us' (Ibid., 89).

References

Barnouw, D. 1996. *Germany 1945: Views of War and Violence*. Bloomington, IN: Indiana University Press.
Friedländer, S. ed. 1992. *Probing the Limits of Representation: Nazism and the "Final Solution"*. Cambridge, MA: Harvard University Press.
Sebald, W.G. 2004. *On the Natural History of Destruction*. New York: Modern Library.

Sontag, S. 1990 (1973). *On Photography*. New York: Anchor Books.
Sontag, S. 2003. *Regarding the Pain of Others*. New York: Picador Books.
Young, J. 1993. *The Texture of Memory: Holocaust Memorials and Meaning*. New Haven and London: Yale University Press.
Zelizer, B. 1998. *Remembering to Forget: Holocaust Memory Through the Camera's Eye*. Chicago, IL: University of Chicago Press.

Chapter 4
The Sound of Silence:[1] Reflections on Bernhard Schlink and Gesine Schwan

For Nietzsche, the cows grazing idly on the grass are to be envied because they live fully in the present. Past failures and successes cannot burden or overwhelm them. Questions of how to free oneself from the past and how to administer justice for past crimes are mute. The present is an eternal now that stretches until infinity. As human beings, we cannot escape our historicity—our very language betrays the fact that we change: I was, I am, and I will be. The past soothes and comforts or it burdens and stifles. Either way, it is an integral part of our individual and collective identities. How then can one find a balance between the past and the present? In his mediation on history, Nietzsche argues for the necessity of a balance between memory and forgetting (Nietzsche 1980: 10). His plea has a particular resonance after the fall of communism as citizens of new democracies strive to make sense of their totalitarian pasts. How can a nation or even an individual acknowledge past crimes against members of its population without incurring revenge? How can one speak about reconciliation without suggesting amnesia?

Bernhard Schlink and Gesine Schwan address questions of guilt, justice, and memory in a refreshing way. Without being moralistic or judgmental in tone, both authors examine how silence distorts relationships on the individual and social level. In different ways, they reflect on the paradoxical sound that protracted silence makes. They analyze how silence engenders distortions of communication. Schlink's lyrical novel, *The Reader* reconstructs the silenced guilt of the perpetrator and the shocked silence of the lover. Schwan's *Politics and Guilt: The Destructive Power of Silence* looks at how silenced guilt affects the political culture of democracy in general and German democracy in particular. What links the two books together is the fact that both authors analyze the synapses and evasions—not of forgetfulness—but of silence between generations. Schlink and Schwan enter into the moral-political swamp of what Hannah Arendt controversially described as political judgment.

The Reader

In *The Reader*, we, 'the readers' are drawn into the narrator's life. Taken in by a woman in her mid-30s when he falls sick walking home from school, 15-year-

---

1 'The Sound of Silence' is taken from the song of the same title by Simon and Garfunkel.

old Michael soon begins an obsessive affair with Hanna that haunts him for the rest of his life. After she abruptly disappears and moves away, Michael returns to his schoolboy life and Hanna is relegated to the realm of a first love. When he next sees her, Michael is a young law student watching the trials of former concentration camp guards and recognizes Hanna as one of the defendants. More than his shock of learning about her past is her growing refusal to defend herself. As Michael listens to her answers, he realizes that she is protecting yet another secret—her illiteracy. Remembering their affair, he recalls that Hanna often asked him to read aloud to her. Reading became a sensual part of their time together. As the trial progressed, Michael pieces together her odd answers to the judges' questions with her attempt to conceal her illiteracy.

If Schlink's account of their affair is filled with poignant tenderness, his narration of Hanna's trial and subsequent prison term is filled with numbness and melancholic detachment. Michael feels betrayed and watches her from a distance while refusing to speak with her. Their affair and her trial became a metaphor for the silence of the war generation and the confused anger of the post-war '60s generation.

> Exploration? Exploring the past!' We students in the seminar considered ourselves radical explorers ... We all condemned our parents to shame, even if the only charge we could bring was that after 1945 they had tolerated the perpetrators in their midst. (Schlink 1997: 91-92)

The process of watching Hanna on trial for not trying to save concentration camp inmates caught in a firebomb, numbs Michael. As a member of the '60s generation, his condemnation of the war generation is complicated by his love for Hanna.

> What should our second generation have done, what should it do with the knowledge of the horrors of the extermination of the Jews? We should not believe we can comprehend the incomprehensible, we may not compare the incomparable, we may not inquire because to inquire is to make the horrors an object of discussion, even if the horrors themselves are not questioned, instead of accepting them as something in the face of which we can only fall silent in revulsion, shame and guilt. Should we only fall silent in revulsion, shame, and guilt? To what purpose? It was not that I had lost my eagerness to explore and cast light on things which had filled the seminar, once the trial got under way. But that some few would be convicted and punished while we of the second generation were silenced by revulsion, shame, and guilt – was that all there was to it now? (Ibid., 104)

As the trial progresses and Hanna is sentenced to life in prison, Michael never contacts her, but is silently tormented and obsessed. 'I wanted simultaneously to understand Hanna's crime and to condemn it' (Ibid., 157). After a failed marriage, Michael begins to read aloud to Hanna again, only this time he records himself reading and mails the cassettes to her. He never writes or calls, but faithfully reads aloud to her for 10 years. Meanwhile, Hanna learns how to read and writes to him, but he never responds. 'I never wrote to Hanna. But I kept reading to her ... Reading aloud was my way of speaking to her, with her' (Ibid., 190). Reading becomes his evasion. His contact with her is both close and removed. It is without risk or confrontation. All this changes when Hanna is granted clemency after 18 years. Afraid to meet her again, Michael puts off visiting her until the last moment. He visits her the week before she is due to be released. Hanna has visibly aged and Michael has difficulty speaking to her. When he arrives the following week to bring her home, she had already hung herself that morning. Her cell is filled with books about the Holocaust among them, Primo Levi, Jean Amery, and Arendt's book about Eichmann.

Schlink's reflections on the love affair between Hanna and Michael are never sentimental or self-pitying. On one level, the book is an attempt to come to terms with Hanna and her Nazi past, but on another level, it seeks to understand how the second generation should remember National Socialism. *The Reader* ends without heroes. It is a painful reflection on the magnitude of crimes of omission. It is also perhaps not so much a condemnation of past crimes—but of poor judgment, of the awful power of silence and the numbed inability to speak.

Politics and Guilt

The private and public silencing of guilt have, as Gesine Schwan skillfully argues, unforeseen reverberations in society. Damaging both personal relationships between parent and child and social relationships between generations, 'silenced guilt' numbs and anesthetizes. *Politics and Guilt* extends the work of Heinz Bude's *Bilanz der Nachfolge* because it examines the social and psychological consequences of Nazism on successive generations. It also complements the work of Martha Minow and Jeffrey Olick by looking at the wider trend of tribunals, truth commissions and other juridical processes of dealing with crimes against humanity (Minow 1998, Olick 2005). Taking her cue from the Polish philosopher, Leszek Kolakowski, Schwan argues for an ethical link between present and past generations.

> The world is an inheritance that we enter upon the day of our birth. At some point, which cannot be pinned down precisely, we come to understand that this inheritance always leaves us a choice: we can reject it by rejecting life. But from the very moment that we know about the possibility of voluntary death and yet go on living, we take on the debts of the world as our own. (Kolokowski quoted in Schwan 2001: 11)[2]

---

2 The quotation is taken from an essay by Kolakowski's entitled 'Ethik ohne Kodex', in *Traktat über die Sterblichkeit der Vernunft, Philosophische Essays*. Munich, 1967, 90.

The idea of an inheritance and debt is connected with the choice of the individual to engage with the world that they are born into. Recognizing each generation's responsibility for the past and future forms the core of Schwan's argument.

Politics and Guilt is strongly influenced by Karl Jasper's categories of guilt outlined in his *The Question of German Guilt*. 'Guilt, therefore, is necessarily collective as the political liability of nationals, but not in the same sense as moral and metaphysical, and never as criminal guilt' (Jaspers 2000: 398). If criminal guilt is linked with established laws, political guilt corresponds to acts of state and invokes ideas of citizenship. Moral guilt is expressed in the individuals responsibility for their actions and negates the justification that an 'order is an order.' Finally, metaphysical guilt is for Jaspers and, I think, Schwan the most important. '*Metaphysical* guilt lays the foundation of all guilt. In its absence it would be theoretically impossible to establish the other, specific forms of guilt' (Schwan 2001: 39). Metaphysical guilt provides the possibility for solidarity and trust in society. Of the four types of guilt, metaphysical guilt is the most central to Jaspers' argument. It is the recognition of the humanity within each person that has been violated during one's lifetime. 'Metaphysical guilt is the lack of absolute solidarity with man as man' (Jaspers 2000: 399). Solidarity has been violated if one is aware of some injustice or crime. Jaspers is stringent in the severity of metaphysical guilt. 'This solidarity is violated by my presence at an unjustice or a crime. It is not enough that I cautiously risk my life to prevent it; if it happens, and if I was there, and if I survive where the other is killed, I know from a voice within myself: I am guilty of being still alive' (Jaspers 2000: 399-400). Metaphysical guilt, as the recognition of one's failure to act as a human being towards another is fundamental for repairing broken social ties and solidarity between individuals.

In contrast to Hermann Lübbe, Schwan argues against the virtue of communicative silence (*kommunikatives Beschweigen*) as a necessary precondition for democracy (Lübbe 1983). Instead, she analyses how silence and 'silenced guilt' in particular damage the ties of solidarity and trust that are the necessary foundation of civil society. For Lübbe, silence provided the context within which individuals could become democratic citizens in the Federal Republic. Schwan finds his thesis unconvincing precisely because, for her, an individual cannot fully change without a minimum acknowledgment of guilt and responsibility. Schwan criticizes Lübbe's split between public and private by arguing that institutions are empty without individual values of solidarity, trust and responsibility. For him, West Germans could only become democratic citizens within a certain period of silence (*gewisse Stille*). If questions of the Nazi past had been immediately raised, the already fragmented and broken individual sense of self would have shattered, further hindering the fledging roots of West German democracy. In a sense, Lübbe makes a pragmatic plea for closure or *Schlußstrich*. Only after democratic institutions are well in place, can individuals afford to ask soul-

---

Schwan also wrote her doctoral dissertation on Kolakowski, entitled, *Leszek Kolakowski: Eine politische Philosophie der Freiheit nach Marx*. Stuttgart: Kohlhammer, 1971.

searching questions of moral responsibility and guilt. 'But unlike Lübbe I want to reveal the destructive—and negative—effect of 'silence,' which extends not only to the generation of the 'perpetrators' but also to their children and grandchildren' (Ibid., 57).

In Schwan's eyes, the privileging of public institutions over individual morality results in lost opportunities for potential learning processes and the establishment of democratic values which bind civil society together and, in turn, nurture democratic and legal institutions.

Unlike Arendt, Schwan maintains that Germans did not lose their conscience during National Socialism; rather many knew that crimes were committed but deliberately avoided self-examination. In an article, 'The Aftermath of Nazi Rule: Report from Germany' originally published in 1950, Arendt describes the peculiar evasions and devices that many Germans employed both during and after the war to avoid seeing the crimes before them. In her opinion, Germans were typified by indifference and self-deception. 'But nowhere is this nightmare of destruction and horror less felt and less talked about than in Germany itself. A lack of response is evident everywhere, and it is difficult to say whether this signifies a half-conscious refusal to yield to grief or a genuine inability to feel' (Arendt 1994: 249). Schwan takes issue with Arendt and argues that Germans never completely lost their morality; instead they simultaneously maintained both traditional morality and a skewed sense of 'Nazi morality' emphasizing the normative values of honor, truth, obedience, efficiency and devotion. 'In contrast to Hannah Arendt and Daniel Goldhagen, I will seek to show that the Germans prior to 1945 had not completely lost their conscience, that all moral traditions had not simply ruptured, and that the Germans did not succumb to hermetic self-deception' (Schwan 2001: 56). Arendt did not see a profound change in Germans before and after the war. Rather she detected a continuity of self-deception that began during National Socialism and carried over into the immediate post-war years. 'But, whether faced or evaded, the realities of Nazi crimes, of war and defeat, still visibly dominate the whole fabric of German life, and the Germans have developed various devices for dodging their shocking impact' (Arendt 1994: 250). In Arendt's opinion, silence did not turn Nazi Germans into good democratic citizens; it merely fostered evasions and escapes from reality. 'The result is that while Germany has changed beyond recognition – physically and psychologically – people talk and behave superficially as though absolutely nothing has happened since 1932' (Ibid., 252).

In *Politics and Guilt*, Schwan also criticizes Daniel Goldhagen's claim that Germans changed from individuals imbued with 'eliminationist antisemitism' to democratic citizens (Goldhagen 1996). For her, one cannot simply assume that all Germans 'willing' abandoned a sense of morality and good conscience to become sadistic murders and antisemites. In her careful examples of not only officers such Eichmann and Stangl, but also 'normal Germans,' Schwan argues that traditional morality co-existed with Nazi morality. She problematizes Goldhagen's facile conception of Germans before and after the war. Although she acknowledges that West Germans certainly did change after the war—Schwan specifically looks at the *quality* of that change and the *costs* of silenced guilt for generational understanding and ultimately for German civil society. After examining religious, philosophical, and psychological conceptions of guilt, Schwan discusses how guilt is necessary for both individual and collective identity. One cannot fully be a person unless one acknowledges responsibility for his or her past. While repression involves a certain acknowledgment of wrong-doing, Schwan's silenced guilt deals with the private and public non-articulation of guilt.

> Thus, "silenced guilt" is not only keeping silent about the clash between actions and norms. It is also, and above all, keeping silent about the inner reasons that gave rise to this clash. It is the refusal to subject myself to an honest self-examination, to bring to mind my freedom and my values and acknowledge my responsibility, to accept my principled capacity for guilt not only rhetorically and half-heartedly but consciously, clearly, and with respect to concrete cases. (Schwan 2001: 82)

She is less interested in the psychological inability of Germans to mourn and more on the consequences of how silenced guilt damages both individual and collective identities.

The most illuminating chapters are perhaps those that focus on the fractured family ties and generational differences in West Germany. There, she argues persuasively against claims for the necessity of silence by examining the destructive ties between the war and post-war generation. For her, silenced guilt was most visible within families. While political elites could publicly admit wrongdoing and administer reparations on behalf of the German nation, there were large discrepancies between the official and private or familial levels of dealing with National Socialism. Here Schwan, in her theoretical reflections converges with Schlink's novel. Silence distorts and deceives. One does not necessarily lie to oneself, but one is also not entirely truthful. Because openness and learning processes are necessary for civil society, guilt should not be silenced but acknowledged. Schwan, however, is not advocating witch-hunts or revenge, but instead offering a sensitive and somber plea for the necessity of openness. In many ways, *Politics and Guilt* illuminates the shock and confusion that Schlink so elegantly describes in *The Reader*. While silence may be the easiest short-term solution, its long-term consequences damage the very fabric of civil society upon which democratic institutions rest.

Schwan illustrates how silenced guilt distorts norms of behavior by citing Hanna's self defense in *The Reader*. When Hanna is asked why she didn't try to save the women locked in the burning church, she fixates on the necessity to do her job, to maintain order, and not to let the women escape. Finally, she looks at the judge and asks him what he would have done in her situation. At that moment it becomes clear that Hanna was incapable of thinking from the standpoint of the women in the burning church. She cannot imagine acting differently. Taken together, Schlink and Schwan's reflections on guilt and silence have an affinity with Arendt's conception of political judgment. Thinking takes place in the world with other people and requires a community or *sensus communis*.

> The power of judgement rests on a potential agreement with others, and the thinking process which is active in judging something is not, like the thought process of pure reasoning, a dialogue between me and myself, but finds itself always and primarily, even if I am quite alone in making up my mind, in an *anticipated communication* with others with whom I must finally come to some agreement. (Arendt 1993: 220)

Judgment, like the acknowledgment of guilt, involves the ability to think from the other person's perspective. One can only do this when the bonds of trust and community are present. If they are fragmented through silence and shock, then political judgment is also hindered. Broken social ties, cynicism, and distrust can only be repaired when guilt for past crimes is articulated rather than silenced. The problem, however of *when* to acknowledge guilt is a delicate one which each individual or nation ultimately has to decide for themselves.

* * *

In a recent series of lectures given at Oxford University, entitled *Guilt about the Past*, Schlink returns to the relationship between guilt and silence that he wrote about earlier in *The Reader*. Reflecting on the role of the Nazi past for his generation, he acknowledges the incompleteness of the past. 'A collective past, like that of an individual, is traumatic when it is not allowed to be remembered, and is just as much so if it has to be remembered. In other words, fixation on the past is merely the flipside of repression' (Schlink 2009: 36). Full mastery of the past is impossible because the past persists in the present. Schlink admits that memories of National Socialism fade with time and that younger generations have a different connection to the war than his generation, or his parents' generation. Even as the Nazi past recedes in importance, it is still bears upon the present.

> What is past cannot be mastered. It can be remembered, forgotten or repressed ... What is done is done. The past is unassailable and irrevocable. The word 'mastering' in its true sense applies to a task at hand that must be worked on and worked through, until it is completed. Then the task no longer exists as such. That the term *Vergangenheitsbewältigung*, i.e. mastering the past, is used and recognized in Germany but has no corresponding word in English and French reveals a longing for the impossible: to bring the past into such a state of order that its remembrance no longer burdens the present. (Ibid., 43-44)

Schlink, like Schwan emphasizes the moral implications of guilt and responsibility for the health of the individual as a moral being and as a citizen. Both suggest that the longer one remains silent, the more distorted and fragmented individual and social ties become. Silence produces its own curious sound or presence that, while not immediately audible, will reverberate in the future. Both associate silence with a deformation of the moral capacity for judgment. In the end, both Schlink and Schwan raise more questions than they answer. However, their writings offer complementary insights into the destructive capacity of silence to haunt present and future generations.

References

Arendt, H. 1993 (1954). Crisis in Culture, in *Between Past and Future*. New York: Penguin Books, 197-226.
Arendt, H. 1994. *Essays in Understanding, 1930-1954*. New York: Harcourt Brace & Company.
Bude, H. 1992. *Bilanz der Nachfolge*. Frankfurt am Main: Suhrkamp.
Goldhagen, D. 1996. *Hitler's Willing Executioners: Ordinary Germans and the Holocaust*. New York: Knopf Press.
Jaspers, K. 1961 (1947). *The Question of German Guilt*, trans. and edited by E.B. Ashton. New York: Capricorn Books.
Jaspers, K. 2000. *Karl Jaspers: Basic Philosophical Writings*, trans. and edited by Edith Ehrlich et al. Amherst, NY: Humanity Books.
Lübbe, H. 1983. Der Nationalsozialism im politischen Bewusstein der Gegenwart, in *Deutschlands Weg in die Diktatur: Internationale Konferenz zur nationalsoizialistischen Machtübername in Reichstagsgebäude zu Berlin. Referate und Diskussion. Ein Protokoll*. Berlin, 329-349.
Minow, M. 1998. *Between Vengeance and Forgiveness: Facing History after Genocide and Mass Violence*. Boston, MA: Beacon Press.
Nietzsche, F. 1980 (1874). *On the Advantage and Disadvantage of History for Life*, trans. Peter Preuss. Indianapolis, IN: Hackett Publishing.
Olick, J.K. 2005. *In the House of the Hangman: The Agonies of German Defeat. 1943–1949*. Chicago, IL: University of Chicago Press.
Schlink, B. 1998. *The Reader*, trans. Carol Brown Janeway. New York: Vintage Books.
Schlink, B. 2009. *Guilt about the Past*. Toronto: Ananasi Press.
Schwan, G. 2001. *Politics and Guilt: The Destructive Power of Silence*, trans. Thomas Dunlap. Lincoln, NE: University of Nebraska Press.

Chapter 5
Living in the Third Person: The Uncanny Hans Schneider/Schwerte

The case of Hans Ernst Schneider/Hans Schwerte is one of those uncanny stories that somehow defies the limits of the imagination and yet at the same time is so utterly normal; one tends to shrug off the strangeness of the tale. The uncanny is something secretive, something that seems familiar and unfamiliar at the same time. In Freud's understanding, the uncanny has a ghostly haunting presence 'Uncanny is what one calls everything that was meant to remain secret and hidden and has come into the open' (Freud 2003: 132).

In the summer of 1992 an American comparative literature scholar, Jeffrey Richards discovered that Hans Schwerte, a distinguished retired professor of German literature and former university rector was actually Hans Ernst Schneider, a senior SS official and a member of Heinrich Himmler's personal staff. After a controversy in German academia and hours before Dutch television was supposed to air an exposé on Schneider's life, Schneider admitted his double identity on April 26, 1995—50 years to the day after he had burned all of his documents. Schneider/Schwerte's radical reinvention of identity in many ways coincided with West Germany's own Zero Hour (*Stunde Null*) as a kind of new beginning from nothing. Likewise, in the wake of unification and the questions of how to come to terms with communism, the double identity of Schneider/Schwerte indicated that not only is the past a foreign country, but also a different person.

Hans Ernst Schneider was born in 1909 in Königsberg, received a degree in German studies in 1928, studied in Berlin, Königsberg, and Vienna and joined the Sturmabteilung in 1933. He worked for the SS-Ancestral Legacy (*SS-Ahnenerbe*), a quasi-scientific occult organization that conformed European culture to Nazi doctrines of race and blood. In 1940 after the Nazi occupation of the Netherlands, Schneider was appointed to the SS-Ancestral Legacy office in the Haag. According to Himmler's plan, the offices of the SS-Ancestral Legacy were to promote terror and propaganda in an effort to force members of occupied Nordic races to embrace their Germanic roots. During this time, Schneider wrote essays for Nazi publications focusing on the German duty to dominate the Slavic race. As he wrote in 1943: 'The sacrifice-ready Nordic race seeks out the tragic fate. Only the Nordic race can experience tragedy. There is no such thing as "human tragedy."' (Schwerte quoted in Allen 1996: 32)

Schneider burned his identification papers on the April 26, 1945 and fled west. He later obtained papers and became Hans Schwerte. He remarried his wife and adopted their three-year old daughter. Leaving Berlin, Schwerte moved to the University of Erlangen in northern Bavaria where he once again resumed his field of German studies. He remained in Erlangen for twenty years as a graduate student and then, later as professor. Schwerte fabricated his new existence with the story that he was forced to quit school in 1937, became a book dealer and from 1939 until the end of the war in 1945 was a soldier defending his country. He received his doctorate in 1948 and his Habilitation in 1958. In 1962, Schwerte published his *Habilitationschrift* in a book ironically entitled, *Faust und das Faustische: Ein Kapitel deutscher Ideologie* (*Faust and the Faustian: A Chapter of German Ideology*). With this publication, he received a warm following among university students. In *Faust and the Faustian*, Schwerte traced the term 'Faustian' from the classical conception of individual hubris to adjective for the German Promethean spirit for knowledge beyond good and evil. As Schwerte himself ironically noted about intellectuals, they are 'on the one hand filled with a sublime aestheticism, on the hand pragmatic to the point of amoral cynicism' (Schwerte quoted in Allen 1996: 36).

Doppelgänger or Life in the Third Person?

In 1955, the West German Federal government issued an amnesty permitting thousands of Germans to resume names that they had dropped due to activities in Nazi Germany. Schwerte, however, decided not to change his name back to Schneider. His transformation from the person of Schneider to that of Schwerte was more radical. His new identity did not entail any traces of National Socialism. In many ways, he went through a private process of de-Nazification. Once Schwerte burned his documents, that past was gone. His dual identity was that of a doppelgänger (Leggewie 1998, Assmann 2006: 141-143). Yet, did Schneider really have two simultaneous identities or trade in an older one for a new one? If he had two selves, then his double was that of a younger self, with a different past, in a different country. However, rather than thinking of Schneider as a double or doppelgänger to Schwerte, we might consider his biography as that of one who lived in the third person. When Schwerte remembered his old self, Schneider—Schwerte lived in the third person. If Schneider had been a Nazi, Schwerte was an entirely different person and had nothing to do with him. In response to accusations of living a double life, Schwerte responded, 'Double life? That's certainly a bit overdone. I have led one life and then another. I have not doubled myself' (Schwerte quoted in Leggewie 1998: 10).

In the novel, *Patterns of Childhood* (*Kindheitsmuster*), Christa Wolf writes in the second and third person—it is only in the last page of the book that she is able to speak in the first person. Accompanied by her daughter and husband, Wolf returns to her hometown in what is now Poland and embarks on a lengthy reflection on her life, the act of memory, and the process of coming to terms with the past. Whereas Wolf could break out of the trap of living in the second and third person, Schwerte seemed to cut himself off from his past and pretend to be a stranger, to be one who, as Simmel noted, comes today and leaves tomorrow. In the opening lines to her novel, *Patterns of Childhood*, Wolf writes:

> What is past is not dead; it is not even past. We cut ourselves off from it; we pretend to be strangers. People once remembered more readily: an assumption, a half truth at best. A renewed attempt to barricade yourself. Gradually as months went by, the dilemma crystallized: to remain speechless, or else to live in the third person. The first is impossible, the second strange. And as usual, the less unbearable alternative will win out. (Wolf 1975: 3)

Living in the first person means a certain degree of agency and continuity. After Schwerte changed his identity, the question of a past no longer seemed to exist. Either he could remain speechless and say nothing, or he could reinvent himself and reinvent his past. Coming to terms with the past meant not forgetfulness, but a radical reinvention in which the past was no longer linked to the present. For Schwerte, the Nazi past was more than a foreign country; it was a completely different person.

After moving to Aachen in 1965, Schwerte became professor of German literature at the University of Aachen and served as university rector from 1970-1973. During his tenure in Aachen, he was a respected social democrat and publicly acknowledged the university's role as a research center during National Socialism. As Schwerte, he did not have a tainted past and was thus able to insist that the university come to terms with its own past. Admired by students during the student protests in the late 1960s and 1970s, Schwerte came to symbolize a solid democrat. In 1983 he received the prestigious civil service cross (*Bundesverdienstkreuz*) from the governor of North Rhine-Westphalen honoring his civil service to the Federal Republic. One could argue that the case of Schwerte confirms Hermann Lübbe's argument that a period of silence was necessary in order for Germany to prosper and become a democratic country. Schwerte's silence about his past was complete and he turned into exactly the kind of liberal democrat that Lübbe invoked as Germany's success story (Lübbe 1983: 2007).

Screen Memories and the Uncanny

Was Schwerte repressing and forgetting his true self as Schneider or was he remembering a different self, the person he wished that he might have been? By taking a new name, he also had to fabricate a biography corresponding to his new self. Freudian attention to the power of unconscious mechanisms of repression, associations, evasions and blank spots are one way of interpreting Schwerte's decision to begin a new life. In reflecting on the difficulty individuals have in recalling their childhood in its pristine entirety, Freud writes:

> It is perhaps altogether questionable whether we have any conscious memories *from* childhood: perhaps we have only memories *of* childhood. These show us

> the first years of our lives not as they were, but as they appear to us at later periods, when the memories were aroused. At these times of arousal the memories of childhood did not emerge, as one is accustomed to saying, but *were formed*, and a number of motives that were far removed from the aim of historical fidelity had a hand in influencing both the formation and the selection of these memories. (Freud 2003: 21)

Certain memories are displaced and others vaguely related to the real event. The compromise between wanting to remember and resistance to memory necessitates a compromise. 'Such a memory, whose value consists in the fact that it represents thoughts and impressions from a later period and that its content is connected with these by links of a symbolic or similar nature, is what I would call a *screen memory*' (Ibid., 15). Memories of Schwerte's past became a screen or covering for Schneider. The only thing that seemed to be common to both egos was the first name, Hans and the fact that the surnames of Schneider and Schwerte both began with the letter 'S.'

> Detailed investigation shows rather such falsifications are of a tendentious nature; that is to say, they serve to repress and replace objectionable or disagreeable impressions. So even these falsified memories must have arisen at a time when such conflicts and the impulse to repression could already assert themselves in a person's mental life – in other words, long after the period to which their content relates. (Ibid., 21)

What makes Schwerte's story so disturbing is its uncanny familiarity. With the change in Eastern Europe from communism to democracy—monuments have been brought down, street names changed or returned to older pre-communist ones. The names of countries and flags have changed; currency replaced—names of universities and ministries changed. The change of names accompanies regime change. The difference though is that the official changing of names in a country did not delete or wipe out the old name. The GDR had a finite life span and was 'reunited' with the Federal Republic—itself a new country after the Third Reich. What made the case of Schwerte strange and uncanny was the element of secrecy in the hiding of his past. As Freud wrote, the uncanny belongs to the realm of the frightening, the familiar and hauntingly unfamiliar. 'There is no doubt that this belongs to the realm of the frightening, of what evokes fear and dread' (Ibid., 123). Looking in German-English dictionaries for the definition of *unheimlich*, Freud notes the associations between that which is haunted and that which is uncanny: 'uncomfortable, uneasy, gloomy, dismal, uncanny, ghastly (of a house): haunted, (of a person): a repulsive fellow' (Ibid., 125). Later reflecting on the linguistic similarity between *unheimlich* und *Geheimnis*, he latches onto the secretive root of the two words. '*Unheimlich nennt man Alles, was im Geheimnis, im Verborgenen ... bleiben sollte und hervorgetreten ist*. "Uncanny is what one calls everything that was meant to remain secret and hidden and has come into the open."' (Ibid., 132) In the case of Schwerte, the secret (*Geheimnis*) of his identity was indeed *unheimlich*. With the uncanny, the line between fact and fiction, biography and fantasy become blurred.

> This is the fact that an uncanny effect often arises when the boundary between fantasy and reality is blurred, when we are faced with the reality of something that we have until now considered imaginary, when a symbol takes on the full function and significance of what it symbolizes, and so forth. (Ibid., 150)

The Banality of Evil

Can one understand the actions of Schwerte as Hannah Arendt proposes that we understand Eichmann—as a thoughtless man who demonstrated the banality of evil? Or was Schwerte merely an opportunist who could remake himself to fit into the new system and was thus a kind of clever survivor? As he said about himself: 'Only now do I understand that I had been skating over thin ice' (Schwerte quoted in Myer 1995: 97) While he did not commit the crimes of Eichmann, some aspects of Arendt's 'banality of evil' nonetheless resonate with Schneider. Her controversial discussion of Eichmann as a man who was not a monster representing pernicious evil but a man who refused to think about his actions seems closer to Schwerte than the metaphor of remorse and forgiveness. As the 86-year-old Schwerte himself declared: 'I didn't hide my identity. I turned it in for a new one' (Schwerte quoted in Allen 1996: 30). It is precisely this turning over of a new leaf, or radical self-revision *without* visible remorse that makes Schwerte so difficult to categorize and understand. Schneider is distinguished by both his distance from his own past and his outspoken public moral stance, against those, who were in the Nazi regime.

Schwerte was master of the *Schlußstrich*. The thick line between his past and present clearly separated his private and public lives. Such a 'radical distancing,' as Leggewie argues enabled Schwerte to learn from history from the sidelines. Schneider was externalized from Schwerte into a different persona and identity. 'He did not lead a double life as a Nazi in democratic clothing; rather he had begun a new life as a reformed (*geläuterter*) person both in private and above all as a public person' (Leggewie 1998: 297). Schwerte was able to speak in the second and third person of 'you' and 'they,' but unable to use the first person singular or plural. Unlike other Nazis such as Eichmann who fled to Argentina and elsewhere to bury their past, Schneider stayed in Germany and remade himself as Hans Schwerte only to later become a successful academic in German studies and an outspoken liberal for the Federal Republic.

For Arendt, Eichmann did not represent a criminal monster but a feeble-minded and thoughtless person who was incapable of distinguishing right from wrong. In her eyes, the counsel and judges missed the point of the trial.

> They preferred to conclude from occasional lies that he was a liar – and missed the greatest moral and even legal challenge of the whole case. Their case rested

on the assumption that the defendant, like all "normal persons," must have been aware of the criminal nature of his acts, and Eichmann was indeed normal insofar as he was "no exception within the Nazi regime." However, under the conditions of the Third Reich only 'exceptions' could be expected to react "normally." This simple truth of the matter created a dilemma for the judges which they could neither resolve nor escape. (Arendt 1993: 26-27)

Arendt's definitions of the normal and exceptional within the Nazi regime are important qualifications for her connection between thoughtlessness, judgment, and the banality of evil. For her, Eichmann was incapable of thinking from another perspective. Judgment requires the ability to think not only for oneself, but to think from another's standpoint. In her *Lectures of Kant's Political Philosophy*, Arendt interprets Kant's Third Critique as a discussion of political judgment. Her reflections on judgment are relevant to her analysis of Eichmann's lack of judgment and inability to think. Thinking requires a community of other people. Likewise, The faculty of judgment requires imagination and reflection. Imagination entails both bringing an object to mind and imagining oneself in another's perspective. Such an ability to imagine oneself from another person's standpoint enlarges our worldview and links individuals into a *sensus communis*. It is only after one has imagined all the possible perspectives in 'anticipated communication' that one is able to reflect and make a moral or political judgment. In Arendt's opinion, what was startling in Eichmann was his complete inability to think from the perspective of anyone but himself. For her, this lack of thought was due not to the monstrosity of his evil actions but to their banality. Moreover, Eichmann claimed to have followed the Kantian categorical imperative and acted out of duty.

> The longer one listened to him, the more obvious it became that his inability to speak was closely connected with an inability to *think*, namely, to think from the standpoint of somebody else. No communication was possible with him, not because he lied but because he was surrounded by the most reliable of all safeguards against the words and the presence of others, and hence against reality as such. (Arendt 1963: 49)

Arendt's much maligned conception of the banality of evil is not intended to lessen the monstrosity of the crimes, but to call attention to the pervasive *Zeitgeist* of not thinking. Acknowledging that it is far easier to imagine Eichmann as a monster, Arendt chose to consider the terrifying normality of individuals such as Eichmann. 'The trouble with Eichmann was precisely that so many were like him, and that the many were neither perverted nor sadistic, that they were, and still are, terribly and terrifyingly normal' (Ibid., 276). The case of Schwerte/Schneider bears a family resemblance to that of Eichmann. Neither man was evil, but plagued by the inability to think about anyone but themself.

Reinvention and Normality

Was Schwerte an accurate representation of many Germans who lived through the war? To what extent, was his identity known, by other members of the university? And in what ways, might he have been protected, by those, with similar pasts? This issue of the relative normality of a man like Eichmann and the complicated levels of Nazi involvement resonate with the case of Schwerte. As head of the SS-Ancestral Legacy's Germanic Scientific Mission, he requested materials for medical experiments carried out for the Luftwaffe by Dr. Sigmund Rascher at Dachau. Although Schwerte's signature was on a request by Dr. Rascher's on January 14, 1943 for medical equipment from Leiden University in the Netherlands, he denied knowledge of the use of such equipment. 'I wore the uniform that stood for unspeakable crimes in Europe. But I myself never killed anyone' (Schwerte quoted in Allen 1996: 41).

In Arendt's opinion, not only were Eichmann's actions disturbing, but also that the fact that his distortion of reality was similar to the immediate post-war years of the Federal Republic. 'Eichmann's distortions of reality were horrible because of the horrors they dealt with, but in principle they were not very different from things current in post-Hitler Germany' (Arendt 1963: 58). Perhaps what makes Schwerte so remarkable is how his reinvention mirrored the radical transformation from Nazi Germany to the Federal Republic. The question is aptly posed by Arthur Allen, in his article on Schwerte, when he asks: '(w)as it the hidden but sincere penitence of a man who assumed that he embodied all that had changed in Germany?' (Allen 1996: 37)

As Claus Leggewie writes in his book, *Von Schneider zu Schwerte*, Schwerte was a 'homo faber,' a man who made and remade himself: He embodied a kind of self-willed blindness allowing him to act like Max Frisch's Gantenbein and create convenient identities for himself. If Schneider would have kept his identity, he could not have continued with a university life. Schwerte's past, as 'Schneider,' was not related to his post-war identity. Instead, his life had normalized. In his opinion, his youthful intoxication and embrace of National Socialism was just that—youthful. By letting Schneider die, Schwerte had de-Nazified himself and turned into a different kind of German. As Leggewie notes, what made the case of Schwerte such an 'irritating lesson' for the German Left was not the way in which he maintained his double identity, but his high stature in West German society and amount of time that he was able to keep his identities hidden. The hidden identity of Schwerte indicated that the categories of 'normal' are dependent upon the one defining them. If normal means not standing out in a crowd, then his dramatic transformation and reinvention were an uncanny example of adapting to a new democratic Germany.

Not only was the double life of Schwerte uncanny; but the vitrolic condemnation by his fellow colleagues bore traces of authoritarianism. Outrage over Schwerte's lie and decision to hide his true identity resulted in the removal of his doctorate, title of professor, Federal Service Cross (*Bundesdienstkreuz*) and dismissal of his university pension. He was publicly condemned for his behavior and his accomplishments as professor, liberal thinker and supporter of students were, as it were, erased by his single decision to reinvent himself. The case of Schwerte was uncanny because he represented two sides of twentieth century Germany: fanatical Nazi ideologue and converted liberal-democrat. As Leggewie argues, Schwerte was a man who wanted to learn from history (*der aus der Geschichte lernen wollte*). In his decision to lead a new life and to teach literature confronting the past, Schwerte had changed. What Schwerte lacked was the public recognition of his self-transformation. "Schwerte had not worked *through* his past (*auf*gearbeitet) coram publico as had been demanded of him; rather he had professionally and in the space of his institutions worked it *off* (*ab*geartbeitet).'[1] Afraid of not being able to lead a normal academic life, he chose to hide his old identity and forge a new one. He changed from *Parteigenossen* to *Bundesbürger* (Lübbe 1983: 2007).

To return to Christa Wolf, perhaps the easiest response to a difficult past is to live in the third person. At the end of Wolf's introspective novel, the author is able to speak in the first person. Interestingly enough, it is not an affirmative clear statement, but rather a hesitant acknowledgment of the limits of self-knowledge. 'And the past, which can still split the first person into the second and third—has its hegemony been broken? Will the voices be still? I don't know' (Wolf 1975: 406). The story of Schwerte reveals the many unforeseen difficulties in changing from authoritarianism to democracy. One cannot simply remove all the citizens in order to begin anew—one has to trust in the human ability to learn from their mistakes. Schneider's second life as Hans Schwerte demonstrated how a private conversion *without* public recognition can backfire and destroy the integrity of an entire life. By distancing himself from the past and living in the third person, the biography of Schneider/Schwerte was an uncanny example of the difficulties in overcoming history and beginning anew.

References

Allen, A. 1996. Open Secret: a German Academic Hides His Past – in Plain Sight. *Lingua Franca*, April 1996, 28-41.

Arendt, H. 1963. *Eichmann in Jerusalem: A Report on the Banality of Evil*. New York: Penguin Books.

Arendt, H. 1982. *Lectures on Kant's Political Philosophy*. Chicago, IL: University of Chicago Press.

Arendt, H. 1993 (1954). The Crisis in Culture, in *Between Past and Future*. New York: Viking Press.

---

1 In the original German, the difference between working through (*aufarbeiten*) and working off (*abarbeiten*) is much clearer. 'Schwerte hat seine Vergangenheit zwar nicht, wie von ihm immer weider gefordert wird, coram publico *auf*gearbeitet, er hat sie aber professionell und im Rahmen seiner Institution *ab*gearbeitet' (Leggewie 1998: 309).

Assmann, A. 2006. *Der lange Schatten der Vergangenheit: Erinnerungskultur und Geschichtspolitik.* Munich: C.H.Beck.
Freud, S. 2003. *The Uncanny*, trans. David McLintock. New York: Penguin Books.
Leggewie, C. 1995. 'Ein irritierendes Lehrstück'. *DUZ: Das Hochschulmagazin*, July 7, 1995, 14-16.
Leggewie, C. 1998. *Von Schneider zu Schwerte: Das ungewöhliche Leben eines Mannes, der aus der Geschichte lernen wollte.* Vienna: Carl Hanser Verlag.
Lübbe, H. 1983. Der Nationalsozialismus im Deutschen Nachkriegsbewusstsein. *Historische Zeitschrift*, 236.
Lübbe, H. 2007. *Von Parteigenossen zum Bundesbürger: Über beschwiegene und historisierte Vergangenheiten.* Munich: Wilhelm Fink.
Mayr, W. 1995. 'Ich bin doch immun'. *Der Spiegel* 19/1995, 94-97.
Wolf, C. 1975. *Patterns of Childhood*, trans. Ursule Molinaro. New York: Noonday Press.

Chapter 6
Goodbye to Grand Narratives? Moving the Soviet War Memorial in Tallinn

During the inter-war years, the Austrian novelist Robert Musil brazenly wrote that, 'monuments are so conspicuously inconspicuous. There is nothing so invisible as a monument' (Musil 1995: 61). Musil is partially correct—monuments all too easily fade into the landscape and are visible for either tourists looking for signs of historical interest or as meeting places for local residents. But what happens when a monument which was once asleep suddenly comes to life and is made painfully visible? Such was the case of the Bronze Soldier war memorial built in Soviet Estonia (1947) to commemorate the liberation of Tallinn by the Red Army. Nicknamed the 'Bronze Soldier' by Estonians and 'Aljoša' by Russians, the Soviet monument stood in the city center amidst apartment buildings, the National Library and a trolley stop. The handsome and melancholic statue suddenly came to life in 2005 sparking heated debates between Estonians and their Russian-speaking minority and in between Estonia and the Federation of Russia. In many ways, the riots surrounding the controversial relocation of the monument to a military cemetery on the outskirts of Tallinn by the Estonian center-right government in April 2007 fulfilled Marx's prophecy that:

> Men make their own history, but they do not make it just as they please; they do not make it under circumstances chosen by themselves, but under circumstances directly encountered and inherited from the past. The tradition of all the generations of the dead weighs like a nightmare on the brain of the living. (Marx 1978: 9)

The clashing interpretations of liberation versus occupation, victory versus trauma, attest to the fault lines in the East European memory landscape. In a resurgent Russia, the Great Patriotic War is an event of mythical importance *separated* from the crimes of communism. For Estonians, however, monuments to that same war are deeply linked to the historical experience of Soviet occupation, deportation and loss of national independence. Two different understandings of the recent past are represented visually in the same war memorial. The conflict over the Bronze Soldier and the riots surrounding its relocation demonstrate that monuments are founded on a paradox. As places of memory, they are supposed to symbolize events from the past for future generations. As works of art, they are supposed to make time stand still. However, since time marches on and societies change, the attempt to freeze time visually into space is fraught with difficulty.

War memorials are cultural symbols reflecting the human instinct for aggression towards one another. While they may have many different interpretations, all war memorials are attempts to make sense of the senseless: violent death at the hands of others. Death is not commemorated due to natural catastrophe or illness, but due to war. Drawing on the insights of Reinhart Koselleck and George Mosse, war memorials are visual representations of the modern nation-state. Divided roughly into three time periods, memorials built before World War I tend to commemorate heroic leaders who died in the name of the nation. After World War I, the democratization of the modern nation-state and national memory accompanied the commemoration of ordinary soldiers—culminating in the tombs of the Unknown Soldier as sacred places of national identity. After World War II, negative or counter-monuments emerged in the West representing military death as overwhelming loss without positing a higher cause to legitimize it. Soviet war memorials, however continued and even deepened the mythical importance of military death as heroic transfiguration in the name of the nation.

When historical events such as World War II are divisive and instill different memories, the past can take on a nightmarish quality that is prone to exaggeration, romanticization and mythology. Furthermore, the past becomes a tool for politicians to play upon the fears and insecurities of individuals reconstructing their social identities in transitional societies such as post-communist Estonia. Former communist societies, such as Estonia are only now free to examine their recent past exposing the different interpretations and memories of World War II, Nazi occupation (1941-1944) and Soviet occupation (1940-1941, 1944-1991). The decision to move the Soviet monument along with the exhumed remains of Red Army soldiers from the center to a military cemetary outside of the city center effectively replaced the narrative of victory over fascism with a more open and universal sentiment of mourning. The symbolic struggle over the meaning of the Soviet monument was more than a sign of local integration problems between Estonians and their Russian-speaking minority and is instead part of a larger reassessment of World War II and the communist past in Eastern Europe. Two memories of the past conflict with one another: an East European (Estonian national narrative) and a Soviet-Russian narrative. If the Estonian narrative emphasizes Estonia as a victim of history and Soviet-Russian aggression, the Soviet-Russian narrative is of Russian victory over barbaric fascism *de-linked* from the crimes of communism. Both narratives are factually true; however as the conflict over the Bronze Soldier monument reveals—the politicization of memory tends to freeze historical events into myth thereby dismissing the complexity of the historical context.

Representing Death in the Name of the Nation

War memorials are about the transfiguration of death at the hands of other individuals. As Koselleck argued, 'dying happens alone; killing another takes two' (Koselleck 2002: 288). Whether figurative or abstract, war memorials are attempts to represent violent death in a rational and meaningful way. They continue the religious (particularly Christian) tradition of martyrdom whereby death is a passageway from one form of existence to another. Koselleck complements Anderson's argument that although the nation emerges with the decline of religion, the social need to provide death with collective meaning does not end, but is instead transformed. 'The decline of a Christian interpretation of death thus creates a space for meaning to be purely established in political and social terms' (Ibid., 291).

War memorials recall military death as 'death for something.' The universal meaning is that death was not in vain but served a greater (often national) purpose. Yet, as Koselleck importantly and pragmatically argues, monuments are built by survivors, in order to commemorate the dead. '(The) establishing of meaning ex post facto can just as likely miss the meaning that the deceased may, if at all, have found in their death. For the death of the individual cannot be redeemed' (Ibid., 288). War memorials are caught in what he calls a 'double process of identification.' The dead are supposed to have died for the same reason that the survivors think they died for. However once a memorial is built, it tends to take on a life of its own: controversial or silent, visible or invisible.

Koselleck's spatial metaphors are helpful in understanding why places of memory such as the Bronze Soldier monument in Tallinn became so politicized. The past is similar to a map or topography onto which historical experiences are captured both visually and spatially in museums, monuments, photographs and film. Thinking of the past as a space of experience suggests completeness while the future is unknown and not yet experienced. Before World War I, memorials commemorated triumphant victory epitomized in the Arc de Triomphe or the Brandenburger Tor. When commemorating national defeat, the monuments tended either to follow the Christian motif of martyrdom or monumental self-sacrifice as exemplified in the Völkerschlachtdenkmal in Leipzig. Military death is not represented as an end in itself, but as a passageway to another state of existence. War memorials commemorate the sacred and mythical origins of the nation. As Anthony Smith argues, memorials to 'the Glorious Dead' are key elements in the symbolic landscape of the modern nation (Smith 2003). Heroic figures tend to easily fade into the background and become part of the public landscape of everyday life.

The Unknown Soldier and the Democratization of Death

The steady increase of war memorials dedicated to ordinary citizens killed in action began with the French Revolution, as the building of monuments became part of the process of nation building. Moving from the realm of churches and cemeteries, memorials have become part of open urban spaces and the public landscape. As a Christian interpretation of death declined, a space opened for political and social understandings of military death. Individual names or the numbers of dead were often inscribed onto the monuments. As differences between class and estates diminished, war memorials increasingly represented what Koselleck calls, 'the democratization of death.' Through military death, even an ordinary persons life gained meaning in the name of the nation.

> Death is transfigured on the basis of individual death for the nation-state so that Tombs of the Unknown Soldier become the highest political symbol. The tombs of the "unknown soldiers" – one for all – are the last steps in this democratization of death. (Koselleck 2002: 317)

Although war memorials have existed since early Greece, Tombs to the Unknown Soldier were built after the First World War (Inglis 1993). As the historian Eric Hobsbawm pointed out, national monuments are firmly rooted in the identity and self-understanding of the modern nation. Indeed the building of monuments is part of the process of nation-building (Hobsbawm 1983).

Because remains from known and unknown Soviet soldiers were buried near the Bronze Soldier in the center of Tallinn, the memorial shares some common features with tombs of the Unknown Soldier built to commemorate World War I. As Benedict Anderson famously wrote,

> No more arresting emblems of the modern culture of nationalism exist than cenotaphs and tombs of the Unknown Soldiers. The public ceremonial reverence accorded these monuments precisely because they are either deliberately empty or no one knows who lies inside them, has no true precedents in earlier times. (Anderson 1991: 9)

The Tomb of the Unknown Soldier is the highest symbolic link between nation and individual death. The reverence given to the Unknown reflects the growing democratization of the nation-state and the ubiquity of death after World War I. Jay Winter and George Mosse have carefully researched the different ways in which the Great War was integrated into a common European narrative (Winter 1995, Mosse 1999). Both emphasize the novelty of tombs of the Unknown in linking military sacrifice and the modern nation. Name and military rank are secondary to the honor of anonymous death. Indeed as Mosse argues, tombs of the Unknown are part of the wider 'cult of the war experience.' Monuments to World War I represent the war with a combination of mourning and heroism. 'The cult of the fallen, in the course of the war, came to symbolize the ideal of the national community as the camaraderie among members of equal status' (Mosse 1990: 95).

The culmination of the myth of the war experience is found in the tomb of the Unknown Soldier. Imbued with pious reverence, tombs of the Unknown Soldier transfer the medieval understanding of death to the modern world. Just as relics (teeth, bones and hair) of saints are entombed in Church altars, so remains of unknowns are buried beneath monuments built in their honor. An eternal flame, symbolizing a life that will never be forgotten, burns eternally before the monument. Depending on the tomb of the Unknown Soldier, there may be a rotation of young soldiers guarding the Unknowns demonstrating both mourning and the power of the nation-state. Unknown anonymous death becomes transcendent: from nothingness and obscurity to eternal sacrifice for the greater good of the nation.

Although France was the first country to discuss the creation of a tomb to the Unknown Soldier, the idea of bringing the remains of an unknown to the national capital occurred simultaneously in France and England. The French Unknown was buried beneath the Arc de Triomphe in 1920. The English Unknown Soldier was taken from a French battlefield and buried in Westminster Abbey on the same day that the French Unknown Soldier was buried beneath the Arc de Triomphe. The overwhelming and senseless loss of military life after World War I heralded a new way of remembering falling soldiers. The Tomb of the Unknown Soldier linked anonymous death with the highest symbolic meaning of national sacrifice. As Mosse notes, 'There was a new consciousness at the war's end that a democratic age had dawned, an age of mass politics, where national symbols – if they were to work – had to engage popular attention and enthusiasm' (Mosse 1990: 96).

Contemporary War Memorials and Moral Trauma

Because trench warfare was the hallmark of World War I, the cult of the fallen soldier was represented in military cemeteries, war memorials and tombs to the Unknown Soldier. World War II though marked a different kind of warfare in which civilian death, genocide and a destroyed Europe overshadowed the death of fallen soldiers. 'The Second World War was a different kind of war that would blur the distinction between the front line and the home front, which knew no trench warfare – so important in the evolution of the myth – and where defeat and victory were destined to be unconditional' (Ibid., 201). Memorials to the Second World War are less about heroic military loss than about victimhood, martyrdom and overwhelming loss. A new genre of memorial emerged in the West with Holocaust memorials commemorating genocide and the loss of a people (Young 1993, Reichel 1995). Such abstract monuments commemorated loss, with an underlying injunction never to forget. Negative monuments reflect on the fragility of memory and the senselessness of human violence towards one another.

In German, *Denkmal* denotes a monument intended for reflection and thought (*denken*). Remembrance (*gedenken*) of the victims includes some kind of empathy and mourning for the victims without trying to identify with them. In contrast, the word *Mahnmal*, often used in reference to Holocaust memorials is a reminder and admonishment (*mahnen*). Such memorials are warnings about the violence of recent history and the possibility for a return to such violence. Unlike war memorials, which represent the violence of soldier against soldier as part of the national narrative, Holocaust memorials are warnings about a deeper break in civilization (Endlich 1995: 16-30). Whereas World War I war memorials could still render military death as honorable, the motif underlying many war memorials in Western Europe after World War II was of incomprehensible senseless death (Koselleck 2001/2002). Debates surrounding the construction of Holocaust memorials, most notably the 'Memorial to the Murdered Jews of Europe' in central Berlin foreground the limitation of artistic representation to fully capture the experience of National Socialism.

> The annihilation not only of the living but also of physical bodies during air raids and even more in the German concentration camps necessitated the renunciation of the old arsenal of forms for war and victory memorials. Victims condemned to senselessness required, if at all, a kind of negative monument. (Koselleck 2002: 322)

Negative abstract monuments intentionally leave a place for individual reflection that figurative heroic monuments occlude. Since death is a private experience, memorials that try to posit a clear identity between the fallen soldier and larger cause might fail. As Koselleck notes, the dead can simply be identified as dead, and often nothing more.

> The only identity that endures clandestinely in all war memorials is the identity of the dead with themselves. All political and social identifications that try to visually capture and permanently fix the 'dying for...' vanish in the course of time. For this reason, the message that was to be have been established by a memorial changes. (Koselleck 2002: 289)

The Vietnam Veterans Memorial: Separating Death from Political Cause

Robin Wagner Pacifici's assessment of the Vietnam War as an example of a 'moral trauma' for the United States is a fitting metaphor for how World War II is remembered in former communist countries such as contemporary Estonia. As Wagner-Pacific and Schwarz argued with reference to the Vietnam Veteran's Memorial in the United States, 'negative events are moral traumas: they not only result in loss or failure but also evoke disagreement and inspire censure? (Wagner-Pacifici and Schwartz 1991: 384). The Vietnam Veterans Memorial in Washington DC in 1982 exemplified a new kind of war monument by *separating* individual death from ideological cause. Built on the private initiative of veteran groups who considered their military service undervalued in American society, the famous black wall of names became 'the wall that heals.' Metaphors of healing a divided American nation and of finding common ground through the universal sentiment of mourning opened up a new space in the vocabulary of war memorials.

Unlike traditional war monuments valorizing death in the name of a unified nation, the Vietnam Veterans' Memorial was able to sidestep legitimating the cause of the war from the loss of human life. The memorial is ambivalent in how it represents the war. It is different from other memorials because it is not heroic; however it fits in with the genre of war memorials by reminding viewers of national loss. In many ways, the Vietnam Veterans Memorial set a precedent against which subsequent war memorials have been measured. The memorial is an example of a postmodern monument that does not judge *how* one should represent the nation: as victorious and heroic or dejected and destroyed. Rather, the names on the wall represent individual death. Death is not abstracted into a higher cause: the dead are not liberators, occupiers, perpetrators or victims—but, simply individuals. The abstraction of the monument rises above political rancor to dignify what all humans have in common: mortality. Maya Lin, the young designer of the monument emphasized that the aim of the monument was to honor loss of life and leave the meaning of that death open to individual interpretation.

> Brought to a sharp awareness of such loss, it is up to each individual to resolve or come to terms with this loss. For death, is in the end a personal and private matter, and the area contained with this memorial is a quiet place, meant for personal reflection and private reckoning. (Lin 2006)

The Neue Wache: Remembering all the Victims of War and Tyranny

Similar to the Vietnam Veterans Memorial, the Neue Wache (1995) in Berlin universalizes death in the 'Central Memorial of the Federal Republic of Germany for the Victims of War and Tyranny.' However, unlike the abstract black wall, the Neue Wache returns to the Christian image of the Pieta. The blow-up of Käthe Kollwitz's private sculpture of a mother holding her dead son became the national symbol for Germany's central war memorial by controversially separating ideological cause from individual death (Inglis 1993, Kattago 1998). Given the fact that Kollwitz's own son was killed in World War I and that much of her art was autobiographical, the image is one of the personal unintentionally becoming political. The mother (who now represents the German nation) is Kollwitz herself. The choice of a Pieta rather than male soldier was deliberate. A mother holding her dead son does not symbolize violence, but rather suffering and mourning.

Likewise, the inscription 'To the Victims of War and Tyranny' did not distinguish between the death of soldiers, concentration camp prisoners or civilians. In the attempt to find a common memorial to represent unified German memory, all victims of war and tyranny were to be remembered in one central location. The site of the Neue Wache was itself historically important because it had gone through numerous reconstructions as a military memorial during Prussia, Weimar Germany, Nazi Germany and communist East Germany. The decision by then Chancellor Helmut Kohl to remake the Neue Wache signaled the historical importance of the monument site as a sacred place of German national memory. Moreover, it was judged to be a fitting representation of both East and West German memories of war and tyranny.

After a long and heated debate about the meanings of the memorial and of twentieth century German history, two plaques were added to the exterior of the Neue Wache memorial from President von Weizsäcker's speech commemorating the fortieth anniversary of the end of World War II on May 8, 1985 (von Weizsäcker 1985). The plaques differentiated the different categories of victims and the historical responsibility of Germany for that loss. With the naming of each category of victim and of National Socialism and communism, an attempt was made to honor the uniqueness of each death. Communism would not be equated with National Socialism; nor a Jew with a German civilian; rather each historical context would be recognized in its uniqueness. The common theme linking all of the dead was one of irrecoverable loss.

The debates in Tallinn about what the Bronze Soldier represented raised similar questions as those surrounding the Vietnam Veterans' Memorial and the Neue Wache. How should military death be represented in a society that is different from the one in which the original monument was built or in which the war was fought? Should Soviet war memorials to the Great Patriotic War be updated to include Estonian occupation by the Red Army? Or does such a change dishonor Soviet soldiers who died in the name of liberation?

Soviet War Memorials to the Great Patriotic War

While abstract monuments emerged in the West after World War II, it was only really in the Soviet Union that the heroic image of the fallen soldier continued. Soviet memorials were mammoth, Social Realist in style and unabashedly heroic. Immediately after the war, memorials such as the famous Soviet War Memorial in central Berlin were built to commemorate fallen Red Army soldiers. Representing heroic transfiguration of death in the name of liberation, muscular soldiers are surrounded by two of the very tanks that liberated the city of Berlin. Graves of approximately 2,500 Red Army soldiers are buried behind the massive memorial. One of the conditions for the removal of Soviet troops from unified Germany was that the German government would maintain and preserve all Soviet-era war memorials. This, however, was not part of the agreement between Estonia and the Russian federation.

In socialist Estonia, as in other communist countries, the ideological doctrine of antifascism was a central justification for the establishment of communist regimes after World War II. As an ideology, antifascism neatly divided the world into two areas of moral and political control: fascist and antifascist (Grunenberg 1993: 120-144). Antifascism was a powerful tool because it was not necessarily a lie, but rather as Tony Judt argued, a kind of mis-memory (Judt 2002). Few doubt the bravery of the Red Army in conquering the Nazis. However, the way in which antifascism was used not only to explain victory, but to shore up the reality of the occupation of Eastern Europe is testimony to the long life span of myth and mis-memory. It was Roland Barthes who most clearly captured the logic behind the power of myth in political life. 'Myth hides nothing: its function is to distort not to make disappear' (Barthes 1972: 121). Myths are mis-memories that simplify and distort the complexities of historical events. Particularly within the complex relationship between the USSR and Nazi Germany, myth simplifies the changing of alliances and the actions of soldiers during the Great Patriotic War. The years when Stalin was allied with Hitler 1939-1941 are not located in the sacred myth of antifascism. It is not a falsification of history, but a complex process whereby antifascism clouds the past so that occupation is mis-remembered as simply liberation.

Although Soviet war memorials commemorate death for the higher cause of defending the Soviet Union against fascist invasion, the monuments are still within the Russian national tradition. The very naming of the war as the 'Great Patriotic War' signified historical continuity of the defense of the Russian people against foreign invasion. Stalin's reference to the war as 'patriotic' (1941) linked it with Napoleon's invasion of Russia in 1812. As Valentin Bogorov argues, Soviet war memorials invoke two cultural sources: a universal classical style of triumph and a Russian imperial tradition honoring the nation (Bogorov 2002). The classical motif of a pantheon is represented in Moscow's Red Square with the entombment of Lenin and carefully tended graves of former Soviet leaders, most notably that of Stalin. Death as heroic transformation is visible with the mummified remnants of Lenin carefully maintained and preserved for public reverence. The war memorials thus establish continuity between pre-revolutionary imperial Russia and the Soviet Union.

> Not only the Soviet Union re-established a symbolic continuity with the pre-revolutionary Russian history, but Stalin firmly situated himself in the context of the Russian imperial tradition. Finally, one may not be but struck at what was missing in the Soviet memorials of this period: the actual memory of the millions, particularly the civilians, who fell victim to the enormous calamity of the war. Far from being concerned with their fate, the first Soviet war memorials had a much different agenda: to celebrate the prowess and the newly redefined image of the Soviet state. (Ibid., 16)

The numerous Soviet war memorials in Estonia commemorate death in the name of victory over fascism. The war that is named and remembered is different in West and East. If World War II is remembered in the West with the years 1939-1945, the Great Patriotic War began in 1941 when Hitler invaded the Soviet Union and the years 1939-1941 when Hitler and Stalin were allied together is not represented in the Soviet memorial landscape. Likewise the independence of Estonia from 1918-1940 is forgotten under the weight of liberation and victory. Immediately after the war, war memorials such as the Bronze Soldier (1947) were built in Estonia commemorating the Great Patriotic War, while Estonian monuments and military cemeteries to the War of Independence 1918-1920 were destroyed and defaced by the Red Army (Erelt 2007).

The Bronze Soldier: Symbol of Liberation or Occupation?

Depending upon who is telling the story: Tallinn was either liberated from fascism by the USSR or occupied by the same USSR on September 22, 1944. The monument conforms to the general model of Soviet war memorials in Soviet city capitals—located in the center and close to Red Army gravesites (Kaasik 2006). According to Soviet archival records, the Bronze Soldier memorial was the burial place of Soviet soldiers who died fighting Nazi soldiers. The Soviets erected a provisional wooden obelisk with the communist red star to commemorate the liberation of Tallinn. An architectural competition for the monument was announced and the choice was made for the current Bronze Soldier mourning for other fallen Red Army soldiers. In October of 1945 a contract was signed between an Estonian architect and sculptor, Enn Roos for the memorial design. By May 1946, young Estonian schoolgirls brazenly shot at and blew up the temporary wooden obelisk. A restored monument was soon erected with 11 known soldiers and no unknowns inscribed (Ibid., 1903).

Legends abound as to who served as the model for the Bronze Soldier statue, but either way rumors concur that the model was Estonian. Some argue that he was an Estonian Olympic wrestler, Kristjan Palusalu. Others point to a worker Albert Adamson, who served neither in the Nazi nor Soviet armies. If it was Adamson, then legend has it that he is depicted as mourning for his own brother, who died fighting on the side of the Soviet army. The monument was completed and dedicated on September 22, 1947 commemorating the anniversary of the 'liberation' of Tallinn. At the unveiling, the Bronze Soldier was officially named 'Monument to the Liberators' (*Vabastajate Monument*) with 11 names and 2 unknowns inscribed on memorial plaques. In 1964, an eternal flame was added before the sculpture. In 1979, the unknowns were identified and a new plaque added listing the names of soldiers buried near the monument (Ibid., 1904). While one might argue that the artistic design of the statue was more mournful than victorious, the monument became a ritualized place to commemorate not only Soviet victory over fascism, but particularly after Estonian re-independence, a place to celebrate the Russian nation.

With Estonian re-independence in 1991, the issue of the Bronze Soldier was not immediately addressed. In 1993, a discussion took place regarding the memorial. A city inspection of the archives couldn't conclude how many people were buried next to the Bronze Soldier monument. The decision was made to preserve the monument, remove the eternal flame and remove the inscription 'Eternal Honor to the Fallen Heroes, who have Fallen for the Liberation and Sovereignty of our Land.' The Soviet inscription was replaced with 'To those killed in the Second World War' in both Estonian and Russian. The new inscription was similar to the Neue Wache because all the war dead, regardless of nationality or ideology were remembered together. Likewise the war was named 'the Second World War' without mention of liberation or victory. In 1995, different proposals were presented to modify the Soviet style of the monument. In the end, nothing happened. Why? One might argue that integration issues in 1995 were more fragile than at present. Furthermore, similar to other East European countries, the goal of European Union and NATO membership unified the society. Since European Union and NATO membership in 2004, questions about how to interpret the communist past have become more prevalent in Estonia and other Eastern European countries. Likewise, the growing assertiveness of Russian nationalism under Putin has created a space where symbols such as war memorials to the Great Patriotic War literally came to life.

With the controversy surrounding the 60th anniversary commemoration of May 9 in 2005, the symbolic importance of the Bronze Soldier increased. Due to clashes between Russian and Estonian nationalists at the Bronze Soldier monument leading up to the May 9 commemoration, it was cordoned off and guarded by police for the summer of 2006. Once the statue was open to the public and no longer under police protection, it was adorned almost daily with flowers and candles. The importance of the monument as a place of Russian national honor and symbol of victory was visible in the active attendance of Russian veterans, schoolchildren from Russian-speaking schools and Russian families. In the winter of 2006 and spring of 2007, a roundtable was formed to study the monument and legislation was passed changing the jurisdiction of war memorials from that of the city to the state (Petersoo 2008: 191-192). This legal change was important because the city of Tallinn has a large Russian-speaking population who favored keeping the monument in the city-center. The center-right government however decided to move the monument and the surrounding remains to a less controversial place. On April 26, 2007, under riot police protection, forensic specialists began to exhume the gravesites and two days of riots followed. On the first evening of the riots, the statue was relocated to the Defense Forces Cemetery on the outskirts of Tallinn.

In its new setting, the memorial commemorates not only World War II with the plaques on either side of the soldier in Estonian and Russian, 'To Those Killed in the Second World War' but also the Great Patriotic War with the headstone 'To the Unknown Soldier, 1941-1945' engraved on black granite before the monument. Like many of the military cemeteries in Estonia, the Defense Forces Cemetery of Tallinn was originally a cemetery for those killed in World War I and the Estonian War of Independence 1918-1920. After 1945, many of the gravesites of Estonian soldiers and monuments to the War of Independence were destroyed by Soviet authorities and reused by the Red Army for their own soldiers. After Estonian re-independence, the British gravesites that were destroyed by the Soviets in the Defense Forces Cemetery were restored and the Russian Embassy financed the black headstone to the Unknown Soldier 1941-1945. In the cemetery setting, the meaning behind the Bronze Soldier is open enough to commemorate both the Great Patriotic War and World War II. Moreover the cemetery setting emphasizes loss rather than victory.

Myths and Memories of Victory Day

The conflict over what the Bronze Soldier should symbolize highlighted the difficulties in remembering not only the war, but also the subsequent communist period. Should war and communism be primarily represented as heroic victory or traumatic loss? The 60th anniversary commemoration of May 9 revealed ambivalent fissures in how World War II is remembered in Europe after the fall of communism. For those countries under Soviet occupation, one could argue that the war really ended when independence was restored and Soviet troops left in the early 1990s. Putin's invitation to participate in the 60th anniversary commemoration of the Soviet victory over fascism on May 9, 2005 sparked heated debate in the Baltics about whether to participate or not. The debates were about the politics of memory both domestically and internationally. The East European experience of communism and occupation clouded the Russian commemorative ceremonies. In the end, only the Latvian president attended the commemoration, while the Lithuanian and Estonian presidents refused to participate (Onken 2007). The absence of the Estonian president only increased the importance of the Bronze Soldier as a Russian symbol of victory over fascism, which was under appreciated by other countries (East European ones in particular).

For Russian national identity, the Great Patriotic War is growing in importance as other Soviet achievements are declining. As Russian social scientist Lev Gudkov writes, 'in the opinion of Russian inhabitants, this is the most important event in their history: it is the *basic image of national consciousness* (*sic*). No other event compares with it' (Gudkov 2005: 5). In response to the question posed in 1996, 'What makes you personally proud of our history?' 44 percent of those surveyed answered the Great Patriotic War. In 2003, the figure was 87 percent. As Gudkov notes, 'there is nothing else left to take pride in: the disintegration of the USSR and the failure of the post-Soviet reforms, the noticeable weakening of mass hopes, and the disappearance of the illusions of Perestroika have furnished the content of traumatic experience of national failure' (Ibid., 5). Attitudes to the war are transmitted through mass media, schools, state commemorations, film and literature. If, as Gudkov argues, Victory Day is the only positive symbol left in contemporary Russia, it makes sense why the war has become such an important point of social cohesion and collective pride.

> Victory does not only crown the war, but as it were purifies and justifies it, at the same time withdrawing its negative side from any attempt at rational analysis, tabooing the topic. It makes it impossible to explain the causes and courses of the war, or to analyse the actions of the Soviet leaders and the nature of a regime that subordinated all spheres of social existence to its preparations for the war. (Ibid., 7-8)

Interestingly enough, growing pride in the Great Patriotic War, correspond to increasingly positive views of Stalin in contemporary Russia: from 19 percent in 1998 to 53 percent in 2003 (Ibid., 8). Gudkov importantly contrasts the commemorative mood of May 8 and May 9. While May 8 is a somber day of reflection in France, Germany and Great Britain, it is predominantly a day of victory in Russia. 'Victory Day has not become a day of mournful commemoration of the dead, the human suffering, and the material destruction. It is literally a day of victory, of the Soviet army's triumph over Hitler's Germany' (Ibid.).

Conflicting Memories of War and Communism

The rewriting of history after 1991 is part of the redefining of collective identities in post-communist societies. During perestroika and immediately after the Soviet Union collapsed, there was a marked interest in dealing with the communist past in Russia. Solzhenitsyn's banned books were published, the citizens' initiative Memorial was formed to remember the victims of Soviet repression and films such as Nikita Mikhalkov's *Burnt by the Sun* (1994) portrayed the terror of the Stalinist years. However, as Tatiana Zhurzhenko deftly points out, interest in the ills of communism quickly waned as the economic and political chaos of the Yeltsin years merged with the nationalism of Putin's government. Democratic open debate about the communist past seemed to undermine Russian national pride. 'But the collapse of the Soviet empire and the subsequent claims of the former satellites and Soviet republics for "victim status" left Russia practically alone with the historical responsibility for the crimes of world communism—a burden too heavy for the post-imperial Russian elites' (Zhurzhenko 2007). Putin effectively normalized the Soviet communist past into Russian nation history. His model of 'sovereign democracy' harkens to a Russian *Sonderweg* or unique democratic path different from that of the West (Ibid.). Furthermore, Putin's remark that the breakup of the Soviet Union was one of the greatest disasters of the twentieth century effectively severed the crimes of communism from the greatness of the Russian nation. The issue of historical responsibility for the consequences of the war was officially dismissed and replaced with mythical heroism.

While Putin-era Russian elites internalize the war as the triumphal foundational myth of the new Russia, the same war represents traumatic occupation and loss of national identity for the Estonian post-communist narrative. The heated debates over what the Bronze Soldier represents in Tallinn are heavily framed within a true/false, national/communist interpretation of the communist past. Reflecting the conflation of Soviet and Russian time, false is defined in Estonia as either Soviet or Russian, while true means Estonian. Likewise, from the Russian side, the war memorial represents the truth of the liberation of Europe from fascism and ungrateful Estonians are cast as fascist sympathizers who falsify history (Brüggemann and Kasekamp 2008, Wertsch 2008).

The restoration of independence, return to Europe, and return to the West were important parts of the Estonian post-communist narrative in the 1980s and 1990s. The Second World War and the Soviet occupation of Estonia are represented as a rupture of Estonian national time. Even colloquial language signifies who owns Estonian national history. The years of independence under the First Republic (1918-1940) are colloquially called 'Estonian time' (*eesti aeg*) and are contrasted with Russian time (*vene aeg*) or Soviet time (*nõukogude aeg*). In everyday language, Russian and Soviet time are interchangeable, while Tsarist time (*tsaari aeg*) is distinguished from Russian or Soviet time. The conflation between Soviet and Russian is an important one reflecting the close association between Russian and Soviet in the Estonian naming of their communist past. The different markers of historical time are testament to Benedict Anderson's emphasis on the importance of measuring time for the modern nation.

> As with modern persons, so it is with nations. Awareness of being imbedded in secular, serial time, with all its implications of continuity, yet of "forgetting" the experience of this continuity – product of the ruptures of the late eighteenth century – engenders the need for a narrative of "identity." (Anderson 1991: 205)

The narrative of identity is one drawing heavily from the past in order to construct a stabile identity in the present. Each occupation of Estonia is accompanied by a different narration of time: from Czarist, Estonian, Soviet/Russian, German, Soviet/Russian, to a re-establishment of Estonian time. Each occupation marks a rupture in the narrative of Estonian national identity.

In her study of Estonian collective memory, Ene Kõresaar argues that Estonian memories of twentieth century history are guided by 'memory pictures' in which the First Republic is idealized and represented in Estonian literature through country life, the thatched roof farm, small villages and intact families (Kõresaar 2005). The farm and village are the images of an ideal harmonious society. The pre-war farm signifies childhood security, social ties and community and is heavily contrasted with modern Soviet society represented by uncertainty, broken social ties and rupture. In oral history narratives, the 'memory picture' of the farm is contrasted with the 'memory picture' of Soviet tanks rolling into Estonia. Memory pictures are ideological pictures or snapshots that crystallize and capture the emotions and feelings of a certain period. Influenced by Maurice Halbwachs' notion that memory is framed by social groups, memory pictures become life ideologies through which individuals narrate their life histories. With such a snapshot understanding of history, time literally stands still. The past becomes mythical and frozen (Halbwachs 1992).

The Soviet rupture of Estonian rural society entailed deportations, destruction of farms, collectivization, and Russification along with dramatic industrialization and urbanization. While the latter two features are common to modern industrial societies, the others remain core features of the Sovietization of society. Kõresaar's work emphasizes the conflict of historical images present in both Soviet and post-Soviet Estonia. Truth meant regaining, restoring and repairing the history that had been taken away by Soviet occupation.

> At the end of the 1980s and in the 1990s when "rupture" as an historical image was being broadly articulated, it was a question of "true" and "false" fact-centered

remembering – by its very existence, a fact contained a meaning which could only be "true" (national) or "false" (communist). (Ibid., 209)

While one can speak of the legal restoration of the Republic of Estonia, contemporary Estonia is ethnically, socially and territorially different from the pre-war Republic. After Russification, deportations and war—the ethnic composition of Estonia has changed from 94 percent ethnic Estonians in 1945 to 61 percent ethnic Estonians in 1989 (Smith 2002: xxiii). Thus the discourse of return encounters the truisms that 'one cannot step into the same water twice' or that 'you can't go home again.' The discourse of return is not only particular to Estonia, but a larger feature of the consolidation of East European democracies (Lagerspetz 1999). By returning to a non-Soviet past, the Soviet past (1940-1991) is externalized in favor of continuity with the time of the Estonian Republic (1918-1940). However, in reality the narrative of return to a pre-Soviet Estonian past is complicated by the integration of Russian speakers into contemporary Estonia.

The current phase of Estonian economic and cultural stabilization is accompanied by changes in the symbolic environment, rapid Westernization as well as weakness in civil society, growing differences in living standards and an ongoing integration of the Russian-speaking minority into Estonian society (Vihalemm and Lauristin, 1997).

Integration of Russians into Estonia produces the unintended consequence of what political scientist, Raivo Vetik terms 'reactive identity' (Vetik 2006). Reacting to the socio-economic and symbolic changes in contemporary Estonia, Russian minorities react by either accepting or rejecting parts of Estonian identity. Reactive identity is most visible in language barriers. Since Estonian is the official language of the country, those who do not speak it are marginalized. Such marginalization contributes to reactive identity, rather than integration. Since Estonians overwhelmingly view the USSR as an occupier, such different understandings of history between Russian-speakers and Estonians indicate parallel societies with conflicting memories of the communist past.

The Unraveling of Grand Narratives

Given the fact that the Second World War is often cast as a struggle of civilization against barbarism, it is not surprising that war memorials are so pernicious. World War II is more of a moral trauma in Estonia because it has different conflicting meanings beyond the liberation of Europe from fascism: Soviet occupation, loss of independence, deportations, destroyed cities, military and civilian death as well as heroic resistance to the Soviet Union among the Estonian Resistance Fighters and the Forest Brothers. How a statue of an Estonian soldier in a Red Army uniform became a heroic cult for many in the Estonian Russian community and Putin's government demonstrates the enormous power of cultural symbols. The Bronze Soldier was neither a clear example of Soviet Realism, nor an abstract negative monument; rather it contained aspects of both. In many ways, it bears more resemblance with Käthe Kollwitz's expressionistic and classical style than with Social Realism. The soldiers' handsome face is poignantly mournful. Victorious heroism was added later with the original Soviet plaque, 'Monument to the Liberators!'

The Bronze Soldier controversy challenged what was politically acceptable as a form of representation. Are there double standards for fascism and communism? For many Estonians, both Nazi and communist regimes were totalitarian because they aimed to liquate the individual through terror and ideology. When social identities are fragile and unstable, the past becomes a treasure chest to be ransacked. The controversy surrounding the 'true' meaning of the Bronze Soldier monument emerged when both sides refused to compromise on a plural understanding of historical truth. Both Russians and Estonians in Estonia link monuments to national identity and national loss: the Estonians to Estonian national identity and the Russian minority in Estonia to Russian and, at times, Soviet identity. Both sides claim a Rankean version of history, 'the way it really was.'

In its new location in a military cemetery outside of the city center, the message is of mourning without glorification of national or ideological cause. In the city center, the monument had two competing meanings: liberation *and* occupation. When solely interpreted as 'liberation,' history was flattened and the fact of Soviet occupation, deportation and loss of Estonian independence forgotten. Likewise, when the Bronze Soldier was only interpreted as 'occupation,' the complex role of the Soviet Army in the liberation of Europe from fascism was downplayed. Moreover, those Estonian men who were conscripted to fight on either the Soviet or the German side were forgotten. While one might argue that the heavy-handed removal of the Bronze Soldier by the center-right government was merely a show of state power to represent national history, it was also an attempt to represent military death in such a way that successive generations could handle and make sense of. By moving the monument to a cemetery, death became transcendent and imbued with respectful mourning. Questions of liberation or occupation were rendered secondary to a seemingly endless litany of continual war. War memorials go beyond individual commemoration because they are sacred places of national honor and mourning. The memorials present a version of history that often borders on national mythology.

The debates surrounding the proper place for the monument demonstrated that grand narratives about winners and losers of World War II are no longer feasible. If anything, the conflict attests to Judt's metaphor about the 'unraveling' of memory in post-war Europe (Judt 2002: 170). The process of change might be slow but there is a shift from post-war to post-communist narratives of the years 1939-1945. Neither the Western narrative about World War II (1939-1945) nor the Soviet narrative about the Great Patriotic War (1941-1945) can fully capture the complexity of those years. The decision to move the monument along with the exhumed remains from the city center to a military cemetery on the outskirts of

Tallinn directly challenged the Soviet-Russian grand narrative commemorating Soviet victory over fascism.

In the cemetery setting, the memorial represents *both* the democratization and silencing of history in contemporary Estonia. It represents democratization, in the sense that narratives of Estonian history no longer need to answer to Moscow. The repressed occupation of Estonia is foregrounded as part of the awful truth of World War II. The cemetery setting also represents a certain degree of silencing in the sense that the vocal opinion of many in the Russian community in Estonia was spatially marginalized from the center to the periphery. Although the Bronze Solider monument may be said to be quietly resting in a cemetery, the conflicted interpretations surrounding World War II and the communist past are still deeply politicized in Estonia and post-communist Europe. As Koselleck suggests, it is impossible for war memorials to completely capture the various meanings of war. The only thing that war memorials can represent with any degree of certainty is death itself, while death 'for something' changes over time.

References

Anderson, B. 1991 (1983). *Imagined Communities: Reflections on the Origin and Spread of Nationalism.* London: Verso.

Astrov. A. 2008. Monumental Crisis: 'Nazis,' 'Occupiers' and Other Nihilists, in *Monumentaalne konflikt: Mälu, poliitika ja identiteet tänapäeva Eestis.* Tallinn: Varrak, 92-111.

Barthes, R. 1972 (1957). *Mythologies*, trans. Annette Lavers. New York: Hill and Wang.

Bartov, O. 1996. *Murder in Our Midst: The Holocaust, Industrial Killing and Representation.* New York: Oxford University Press.

Bauman, Z. 1989. *Modernity and the Holocaust.* Ithaca, NY: Cornell University Press.

Bogorov, V. 2002. In the Temple of Sacred Motherland: Representations of National Identity in the Soviet and Russian WWII Memorials. Available at http://www.dartmouth.edu/~crn/groups/geographiers_group_papers/Finalpapers/Bogorov02.pdf. Accessed September 20, 2008.

Brüggemann, K. and Kasekamp, A. 2008. The Politics of Memory and the 'War of Monuments' in Estonia. *Nationalities Papers*, 36:3, July, 425-448.

Endlich, S. and Lutz, T. 1995. *Gedenken und Lernen an Historischen Orten: Ein Wegweiser zu Gedenkstätten für die Opfer des Nationalsozialismus in Berlin.* Berlin: Landeszentrale für politische Bildungsarbeit.

Erelt, P. 2007. Kui monumente teisaldati dünamiidiga. (When Monuments are Relocated with Dynamite) *Eesti Ekspress*, January 30. Available at www.ekspress.ee/print/266851090B9FC7C2257273003A71EA. Accessed March 15, 2007.

Grunenberg, A. 1993. *Antifaschismus: Ein deutscher Mythos.* Hamburg: Rowohlt.

Gudkov, L. 2005. The Fetters of Victory. How the War provides Russia with its Identity. *Osteuropa* 4-6. Accessed in *Eurozine*, March 13, 2007. Available at www.eurozine.xom/articles/2005-05-03-gudkov-en.html, 5.

Halbwachs, M. 1992. *On Collective Memory*, trans. Lewis A. Coser. Chicago, IL: University of Chicago Press.

Hobsbawm, E. 1983. *The Invention of Tradition*. Cambridge: Cambridge University Press.

Inglis, K. 1993. Grabmäler für Unbekannte Soldaten in *Die Neue Wache Unter den Linden: Ein Deutsches Denkmal im Wandel der Geschichte*. Berlin: Koehler & Amelang, 150-171.

Judt, T. 2002. The Past is Another Country: Myth and Memory in Post-war Europe, in *Memory and Power in Post-War Europe*, edited by Jan-Werner Müller, London: Cambridge University Press, 157-183.

Kaasik, P. 2006. Tõnismäe pronkssõdur, *Akadeemia*, 18:9, 1891-1918.

Kattago, S. 1998. Representing German Victimhood and Guilt: The Neue Wache and Unified German Memory. *German Politics and Society* 16:3, 86-104.

Koselleck, R. and Jeismann, M., eds. 1994. *Der politische Totenkult: Kriegerdenkmäler in der Moderne*. Munich: Wilhelm Fink Verlag.

Koselleck, R. 1993. Bilderverbot, in *Die Neue Wache unter den Linden: Ein deutsches Denkmal im Wandel der Geschichte*, edited by Christoph Stölzl. Berlin: Koehler & Amelang, 200-203.

Koselleck, R. 2001/2002. Die Transformation der Politischen Totenmale im 20. Jahrhundert. *Transit: Ein europäisches Revue*, number 22, Winter 2001/2002, 59-86.

Koselleck, R. 2002. *The Practice of Conceptual History: Timing History, Spacing Concepts*, trans. Todd Samuel Presner. Palo Alto, CA: Stanford University Press.

Kõresaar, E. 2005. *Elu Ideoloogiad: Kollektiivne mälu ja autobiograafiline minevikutõlgendus eestlaste elulugedes*. (*Ideologies of Life: Collective Memory and Autobiological Meaning-Making of the Past in Estonian Life Stories*). Tartu: Eesti Rahva Muuseum.

Lagerspetz, M. 1999. Postsocialism as a Return: Notes on a Discursive Strategy. *East European Politics and Societies*, 13:2, 377-390.

Lin, M. 2006. Available at www.vvmf.org/POPUP_printing.cfm?sectionID=77, October 23.

Marx, K. 1978 (1852). *The Eighteenth Brumaire of Louis Bonaparte*, Peking: Foreign Languages Press.

Mosse, G.L. 1990. *Fallen Soldiers: Reshaping the Memory of World Wars*. Oxford: Oxford University Press.

Musil, R. 1995. Monuments in *Posthumous Papers of a Living Author*, trans. Peter Wortsman, New York: Penguin, 61-64.

Onken, E.C. 2007. The Baltic States and Moscow's 9 May Commemoration: Analysing Memory Politics in Europe. *Europe-Asia Studies*, 59:1, January, 23-46.

Reichel, P. 1995. *Politik mit der Erinnerung: Gedächnisorte im Streit um die nationalsozialistische Vergangenheit.* Munich: Carl Hanser Verlag.

Smith, D. 2002. Estonia: Indendence and European Integration, in *The Baltic States: Estonia, Latvia and Lithuania,* edited by M. Lehti and D.J. Smith. London: Routledge.

Smith, A.D. 2003. *Chosen Peoples: Sacred Sources of National Identity.* Oxford: Oxford University Press.

Stölzl, C. ed. 1993. *Die Neue Wache unter den Linden: Ein Deutsches Denkmal im Wandel der Geschichte.* Berlin: Koehler & Amelang.

Vetik, R. 2006. Reactive Identity versus EU Integration. *JCMS,* 44:5, 1079-1102.

Vihalemm, T. and Lauristin, M. 1997. Cultural Adjustment to the Changing Societal Environment: The Case of Russians in Estonia in *Return to the Western World,* Tartu: Tartu University Press, 279-297.

Von Weizsäcker, R. 1985. Speech by Richard von Weizsäcker, President of the Federal Republic of Germany, in the Bundestag during the Ceremony Commemorating the 40th Anniversary of the End of the War in Europe and of National Socialist Tyranny, May 8, 1985 in *Bitburg in Moral and Political Perspective,* edited by Geoffrey Hartman. Bloomington, IN: Indiana University Press, 263-273.

Wagner-Pacifici, R. and Schwartz, B. 1991. The Vietnam Veterans Memorial: Commemorating a Difficult Past. *American Journal of Sociology* 97, September, 376-420.

Wertsch, J. 2008. Collective Memory and Narrative Templates. *Social Research* 75:1, Spring, 133-156.

Winter, J. 1995. *Sites of Memory, Sites of Mourning: The Great War in European Cultural History.* Cambridge: Cambridge University Press.

Young, J.E. 1993. *The Texture of Memory: Holocaust Memorials and Meaning,* New Haven, CT: Yale University Press.

Zhurzhenko, T. 2007. The Geopolitics of Memory. *Transit,* 10 May, 2007. Available at www.eurozine.com/articles/2007-05-10-zhurzhenko-en.html. Accessed September 12, 2008.

Chapter 7
Memory, Pluralism and the Agony of Politics

Recent debates in Estonia surrounding the Bronze Soldier monument touch a core issue for democratic societies: how to recognize different interpretations of the past without falsifying history. Liberal democracies, both old and new, are faced with the question of how to reconcile many different and even conflicting memories of the past. In the case of the Baltics States, two narratives of the recent past perennially conflict with one another: whether the war and the subsequent communist period should be remembered primarily as occupation or liberation. Beneath the surface often lie hardened stereotypes, resentment, misunderstandings and accusations of collective guilt. If, for example, the Estonian national narrative highlights the Estonian nation as a victim of dual occupations by Nazi Germany and the Soviet Union, the Soviet-Russian narrative emphasizes the USSR as the liberator of Europe from fascism and the willing annexation of the Baltic States to the USSR. Given the fact that 60 years have passed since the end of the war, one may wonder why the past so easily becomes a weapon to be crudely used against one another.

The very meaning of democracy is challenged when different groups link their core identity to ethnic or national memories. The politicization of the past in Estonia challenges how democracy as both a set of institutions and as a way of life is understood. Labeling all Estonians as fascists and all Russians as occupiers misses what they historically share in common: experience of living under the totalitarian regime of the Soviet Union. If memories of the past are divisive, a Schmittian conception of politics as 'us-versus-them' is quickly engaged. Such a romanticization of antagonistic conflict lessens the chances for mutual respect and toleration. Likewise, an overly procedural model of democracy is not attentive enough to the important role of history and memory in identity formation. A re-thinking of pluralism by Hannah Arendt and Isaiah Berlin offers a more nuanced understanding of democratic politics. One needs to take seriously the different interpretations of history that influence collective identity. Democracy is less about consensus than about *how* individuals deal with difference within a given polity. The first step towards pluralism is a wider understanding of democratic participation emphasizing mutual respect, rather than impenetrable difference. If we are to take pluralism seriously, then total consensus about the past is impossible and, perhaps even undesirable.

Democratic Paradox: E pluribus unum

Modern democracy is built upon an old philosophical paradox: the reconciliation of the many and the one. In other words, what is the fairest and most open way to reconcile the opinions of many different citizens into the common will of the majority? If modern liberalism emphasizes the rights of the autonomous individual, communitarians are more attentive to how individuals are influenced by culture, history and ethnic difference. For Chantal Mouffe (2002), liberalism mistakenly tries to eliminate antagonism from politics. Relying on Carl Schmitt's critique of liberalism, Mouffe argues for a radical democracy that returns antagonism to the center of politics. Disappointed in the deliberative procedural model of democracy articulated by Rawls, Habermas and Dworkin, Mouffe's starting point for a revitalization of democracy is Schmitt's adversial understanding of politics. For Schmitt, the political 'can be understood only in the context of the ever present possibility of the friend and enemy grouping, regardless of the aspects which this possibility implies for morality, aesthetics and economics' (Schmitt 1979 [1923]: 35).

In many ways, Mouffe has an important point—antagonism is central to politics. However, by invoking Schmitt, politics embraces a Manichean division of the world into 'us' versus 'them.' When memories of the past are politicized, they often split into two opposing sides. For Mouffe, the liberal 'denial of antagonism is what prevents liberal theory from understanding democratic politics' (2002: 5). She cautions that if the left ignores emotions, passions and the friend/enemy model of identification—the political will fall prey to right-wing populism and extremism. Here again, Mouffe makes a serious point. To ignore *how* memories of the past are emotionally and existentially linked to collective identity does not solve conflict, but rather wishes it away. The controversy in Estonia surrounding the different meanings of the Bronze Soldier monument was an apt example of Mouffe's antagonistic politics played out in moral terms of good and evil, winner and loser, liberator and occupier, communist and fascist. When government officials ignore the resentment and sense of exclusion underlying conflict the antagonistic model of politics is ironically re-inforced. If both sides see the other solely as a foe or adversary, the 'us-versus-them' model is locked into place, silencing any real possibility for discussion, toleration and potential compromise.

What is missing from Schmitt and Mouffe is the possibility—however slight—for some degree of respect between people. Some mutual respect is needed for the recognition and tolerance of different understandings of history. Respect for the uniqueness of the individual forms the core of Hannah Arendt's politics. Already from her dissertation on St. Augustine to her book, *The Human Condition*, until one of her last posthumously published essays 'Introduction into Politics,' Arendt emphasized the importance of human plurality, new beginnings and uniqueness. 'Politics is based on the fact of human plurality. God created *man*, but *men* are a human, earthly product, the product of human nature' (Arendt 2005: 93). In contrast to Mouffe and Schmitt, Arendt's conception of the political is *both* agonal and discursive. Arendt's public sphere contains aspects of debate and antagonism, compromise and unresolvable conflict. If the Schmittian concept of the political posits endless antagonism, Arendt puts freedom at the center of politics. Freedom is the space between individuals. It is linked with new beginnings and a deep appreciation of pluralism as a value in itself. 'Freedom exists only in the unique intermediary space of politics' (Arendt 2005: 95). If Schmitt reduces politics to antagonism between two players, Arendt's polis is a lively town hall debate of multiple players, partial agreement, theatrical performance and impassioned discussion.

For Arendt, 'human plurality is the paradoxical plurality of unique being' (1958: 176). Each person, by the very fact of his/her birth, is unique. Although individuals share their humanity in common, each person is distinct from others. 'Plurality is the condition of human action because we are all the same, that is, human, in such a way that nobody is ever the same as anyone else who ever lived, lives, or will live' (Ibid., 8). The democratic promise is based upon the possibility of individual change. Because each person possesses the capacity for change, freedom becomes the most important element of politics. 'With the creation of man, the principle of beginning came into the world itself, which, of course, is only another way of saying that the principle of freedom was created when man was created but not before' (Ibid., 177). Arendt's conceptions of natality and new beginnings overcome the antagonistic impasse of Schmitt and Mouffe. Indeed, Arendt's interpretation of the ancient Greeks polis highlights how it operates *within* the tension of discourse and antagonism (Benhabib 1990). While Mouffe and Schmitt emphasize two eternally opposing sides, Arendt's pluralism suggests that conflict is multiple and plural rather than dual. 'Politics deals with the coexistence and association of *different* men. Men organize themselves politically according to certain essential commonalities found within or abstracted from an absolute chaos of differences' (Arendt 2005: 93).

Trauma and Collective Guilt

Particularly in the Baltic States, where Balts are often cast as 'victims' of communist occupation and Russian-speakers as 'occupiers,' the past quickly becomes politicized and polarized. In many ways, what seems to be happening in the Baltics is not entirely unique but part of an unraveling of East and West narratives about the war and the ideological division of Europe. As Tony Judt argues, the post-war years and memories of World War II quickly split into the narrative structure of victims and perpetrators. 'Two moral vocabularies, two sorts of reasoning, two different pasts' (Judt 2002: 163). If, as Judt notes, Western Europe suffers from too little memory and a veritable, even comfortable sense of amnesia, Eastern Europe suffers from too much memory. 'Here there is too much memory, too many pasts on which people can draw, usually as a weapon against the past of someone else' (Judt 2002: 172). Judt cautions against recalling the past through the lens of victim or perpetrator. Such identification leaves little room for the larger cast of those who worked for the communist state, those who for different reasons were bystanders and collaborators. If victim and perpetrator or victim and occupier are the categories through which history is written, the complexity of the past is flattened and made into a kind of moral drama harboring mis-memories and myths. Judt's metaphor of East European memory as an archipelago helps to elucidate why history is often wielded as a weapon in places such as the Baltic States. 'For Eastern Europeans the past is not just another country, but a positive archipelago of vulnerable historical territories, to be preserved from attacks and distortions perpetratred by the occupants of a neighboring island of memory…' (Judt 2002: 172).

Merging with the identity politics of the 1990s, emphasis on ethnic or national trauma encourages the antagonism of 'us versus them.' When memories attain a 'sacred status,' it becomes more difficult for historians to research the events (Misztal 2005: 1321, Misztal 2004). If, for example, May 9 is only remembered as 'victory' and is increasingly viewed as holy in contemporary Russia, East European memories of that same 'victory' are forgotten. Likewise, if Baltic memories of 'occupation' become sacred, it discourages historical research into those local Baltic communists, who may have also served in the regime. Avashai Margalit's thesis that an ethics of memory is connected with a traumatic past is relevant in the Baltics (Margalit 2002). The trauma of occupation and deportation is remembered with an ethical injunction 'never to forget.' Represented in school textbooks, museums of occupation in each of the Baltic countries, and national days of remembrance, the trauma of communism is a central motif accompanying the long desire for freedom and national independence. Similarly, the Russian trauma of suffering during the Great Patriotic War that the West sorely underestimates is also cast with an injunction to remember. From recent Russian history textbooks revering Stalin to the renewed importance surrounding the commemorative ceremonies of Victory Day—the suffering of the Russian people is sacred (*The Economist* 2007). In both cases, the sacralization of trauma can just as well lead to national cohesion as to resentment and endless antagonism.

> Trauma, like a covered stain, still has effects. It makes the traumatized person react disportionately to a present trigger on the strength of the injury from from the past. Or it displaces that which brought the trauma about with a different object that is somehow associated with the object of the past. (Margalit 2002: 126)

Narratives of return to Europe and nationhood after the dark years of communist occupation are a common theme in the post-communist landscape (Lagerspetz 1999, Outhwaite/Ray 2005). The problem arises when Russian-speakers are cast as occupiers and Soviets. When the traumatic memory of deportation and occupation suggests that *all* Russians, because of their nationality are collectively guilty for the crimes of communism, the memory unfairly silences those who might have acted differently. Likewise, labeling *all* Estonians or Latvians as fascists because some soldiers fought on the Nazi side crudely twists historical complexity into stereotypes. Rather than emphasize the common experience of living in a communist society, differences are highlighted along national and ethnic lines. While the differences are important, the problem arises when entire nations rather than their governments are held responsible for crimes committed in the name of the nation. As Arendt wrote with respect to Germany,

> There is such a thing as responsibility for things one has not done; one can be held liable for them. But there is no such thing as being or feeling guilty for things that happened without one's actively participating in them... Where all are guilty, nobody is. (2003: 147)

Pluralism and the Open Society

In his reflections of the democratic revolutions in Eastern Europe written in the form of a 'letter to a gentleman in Warsaw,' Ralf Dahrendorf argued that what unites the various revolutions is a desire to live in an open society. How this openness will be interpreted and discovered will be different in each nation.[1]

> If any creed has won in the events of last year, it is the idea that we are all embarked on a journey into an uncertain future and have to work by trial and error within institutions which make it possible to bring about change without bloodshed. What has died in the streets of Prague and Berlin and Bucharest, in the endless meetings of Budapest, on your Round Table and now in your parliament, is not just communism, but the belief in a closed world, which is governed by a monopoly of 'truth.' (Dahrendorf 1990: 35)

Invoking the ideas of Karl Popper, Dahrendorf argues that the foundation of a liberal democracy is openness and the possibility of many, perhaps evening competing truths (Popper 1966 [1945]). Central to the idea of an open society is a belief in the possibility of individuals *to learn* from their mistakes and to change.

> There is no greater danger to human liberty than dogma, the monopoly of one group, one ideology, one system. By the same token, the greatest task is to keep our affairs open for change. The open society does not promise an easy life. Indeed human beings have a dangerous penchant for the coziness of a closed world. But if we want to move forward and improve ourselves and the conditions in which men and women live on this planet, we have got to accept

---

[1] Modeled on Edmund Burke's *Reflections on the Revolution in France*, Dahrendorf's prescient reflections were written in the form of a letter. However, unlike Burke, Dahrendorf reflected on the positive aspects of the East European revolutions.

the untidy, antagonistic, uncomfortable, but proud and encouraging prospect of open horizons. (Dahrendorf 1990: 24-25)

What distinguishes Dahrendorf's understanding of democracy from that of Mouffe is the possibility for an 'open horizon.' Dahrendorf, Popper, Berlin and Arendt all include antagonism as an important part of democratic politics—but they do not romanticize conflict as the essence of the political. In *The Democratic Paradox*, Mouffe suggests that democracy should be understood not as deliberation or pluralism, but as agonistic pluralism. 'I see the category of "the adversary" as the key to envisage the specificity of modern pluralistic democratic politics, and it is at the very centre of my understanding of democracy as "agonistic pluralism"' (2000: 14). Mouffe distinguishes her antagonistic pluralism from Arendt's conception of the political by arguing that Arendt invokes 'agonism without antagonism' (Mouffe 2007: 4). Because Mouffe emphasizes that conflict should not be silenced to the private realm and highlights the importance of emotions as driving forces of individual action, conflict gains a kind of sacred quality. Indeed Mouffe argues, that 'Arendt, like Habermas ends up envisaging the public sphere in a consensual way' (Ibid.).

A society that is open to criticism and self-reflection is accompanied by a certain degree of untidiness. One cannot explain every aspect of the past; however, in the process of trying to understand, one should also try to listen to what others say. Openness to others demands a wider conception of historical truth that is only possible in an open society. A closed society such as the Soviet Union only allowed one official truth, with private memories forced underground. An open society does not mean living in a lie, nor does it mean historical relativism. Rather, it means that history is far more difficult to represent than a single monolithic notion of truth. If one takes pluralism seriously, how can one avoid the relativism that anything goes? Pluralism and freedom of speech suggest that narratives about the past should be open to citizens, civic organizations and political representatives of government. Given this plurality of voices, how then can one distinguish between true and false stories? How can one prevent revisionism and a whitewashing of the past?

An open society values pluralism for the simple reason that each individual is unique. While pluralism emphasizes the particular context of individuals, it is not the same as relativism. The foundation of an open society is pluralism, while a closed society is based on monism or the belief in one truth. Isaiah Berlin outlines that pluralism implies mutual respect for different cultures and different ideas of the good. However, what links individuals together is that pluralism itself is a *shared* value. Here, it is interesting to note that Berlin himself had many identities: Russian-Jew born in Riga, naturalized citizen of the UK, and perhaps most importantly, fellow of the University of Oxford. 'The enemy of pluralism is monism—the ancient belief that there is a single harmony of truths into which everything, if it is genuine, in the end must fit' (Berlin 1998: 14). Taking his cue from Italian philosopher Giambattista Vico, Berlin argues that culture and historical context invariable influence what individuals deem to be true. However, the quest for a single truth that is universally accepted is monistic and based on the premise of silencing those who disagree. In his plea for pluralism, Berlin suggests a view of democracy less as consensus, and more as the civility to disagree. Individuals can disagree on what history means or how historical events are interpreted. The trick is to try and find points of common interest while politely disagreeing on areas of conflict. If relativism would posit that any agreement does not matter, pluralism is based upon a minimum liberal agreement of decency, individual respect and the value of human dignity. Individuals are not determined by their cultures and insulated from finding some degree of common understanding. But at the same time, one can and should not discount the important role that culture plays in the outlook of each individual. Imaginative insight, or what Vico calls *fantasia*, can provide opportunities for understanding and empathy with others (Vico 1948). Here, Berlin's emphasis on 'imaginative insight' complements Arendt's pluralism and 'enlarged mentality.' Pluralism entails the ability and desire to think from different perspectives. As Andrew Schaap argues in his discussion of Mouffe and Arendt, while both thinkers include conflict into the political, they interpret its significance differently. The importance of conflict for Mouffe is 'that it makes available meaningful choices that could engage the demos in political life, for Arendt the significance of the conflict lies in its potential to disclose the commonness of a social world to those it draws in' (Schaap 2007: 3). It is a difficult balance to maintain the competitive nature of the agon without sliding into what Schaap terms, 'the agony of politics.' Although individuals can never completely understand one another, they can and *should* try to think from the perspective of the other. Mouffe, like Schmitt dismisses this possibility as idealistic and wrong-headed. However, politics that is viewed primarily through the prism of everlasting conflict feeds into an either/or monistic understanding of the world. As Berlin carefully argues, monism is constricted by the narrowness of its own self-proclaimed truth. Monism is blind to an alternative understanding of experience, or as Arendt, invoking Immanuel Kant would say, a *sensus communis* and enlarged mentality (Arendt 1982: 68-77).

Like Herder, Berlin argues for the importance and incommensurability of cultures. Each nation and culture should be appreciated on its own merit, rather than measured against one another. 'Each nation has its own *center* of happiness *within itself,* just as every sphere has its own center of gravity' (Herder 1993: 43). A single concept of truth is linked to the closed society, while an open pluralistic society entails many, even conflicting truths. 'The notion of the perfect whole, the ultimate solution, in which all good things coexist, seems to me to be not merely unattainable—that is a truism—but conceptually incoherent; I do not know what is meant by harmony of this kind' (Berlin 2003: 13). If one values pluralism, decency follows. The best one can hope for is to avoid 'extremes of suffering.' Here Berlin comes remarkably close to Richard Rorty's plea for a liberal utopia in which the goal should be less cruelty in the world rather than more (Rorty 1989). Less suffering entails trade-offs. Drawing from utilitarianism and pragmatism, pluralism seeks to avoid violent conflict over principles and ideas by seeking pragmatic compromise.

> If pluralism is a valid view, and respect between systems of values which are not necessarily hostile to each other is possible, then toleration and liberal consequences follow, as they do not either from monism (only one set of values is true, all the others are false) or from relativism (my values are mine, yours are yours, and if we clash, too bad, neither of us can claim to be right). (Berlin 1998: 13)

Since we cannot choose our ethnicity or nationality, but rather are born into them—one should be cautious about making a virtue out of necessity. While each culture is unique, it does not follow that they are closed to foreigners and that we can never find common grounds of understanding due to our cultural differences. Neither Arendt's nor Berlin's pluralism equals relativism. In a pluralist society, toleration and empathy are shared values, albeit with important nuances. Living in a democracy means that individuals possess the potential for tolerance and empathy. Consensus is not possible on all issues, nor is it particularly desirable because political debate is the heart of democracy. 'That is why pluralism is not relativism – the multiple values are objective, part of the essence of humanity rather than arbitrary creations of men's subjective fancies' (Berlin 1998: 12). Pluralism, in the sense of Arendt and Berlin, is based upon a deep appreciation of the dignity of humanity. Tradition and history inevitably influence the perspective of individuals; likewise there exist a multitude of truths. 'Intercommunication between cultures in time and space is only possible because what makes men human is common to them, and acts as a bridge between them' (Berlin 2003: 11).

Just as the open society seeks to avoid the dogma of monism, so a plurality of memories entails some degree of official recognition of different stories about the past. As Taylor, Habermas and Honneth have argued, albeit in different ways, official recognition of different cultural traditions by the state is a central challenge for democracies. The democratic promise is that the many voices have freedom of expression, have the right to be heard and recognized whether in schoolbooks, museums, commemorations or parliamentary politics. As recent politics in Estonia has demonstrated, the difficulty arises with the official recognition of different interpretations of the past. All too quickly, *demos* slides into *ethnos* and the agony of politics is invoked over a more discursive pluralistic model.

Learning from History, Not Returning to it

Rather than returning to a mythical or traumatic past, it might be wise to reflect on the oft-quoted words of George Santayana. 'Those who cannot remember the past are condemned to repeat it' (Santayana 1998: 82). The point is not to pour salt into old wounds but rather to learn from history—so as not to make the same mistakes in the future. Understanding requires empathy, tolerance of difference and, as Isaiah Berlin wryly notes, a certain degree of humility.

> The best that can be done, as a general rule, is to maintain a precarious equilibrium that will prevent the occurance of desperate situations, of intolerable choices – that is the first requirement for a decent society; one that we can always strive for, in the light of the limited range of our knowledge, and even of our imperfect understanding of individuals and societies. A certain humility in these matters is very necessary. (Berlin 2003: 17-18)

The question of whether memory or forgetfulness is a necessary condition for a just and decent democratic society has been raised with particular urgency since the Nuremberg trials. It implies that governments bear responsibility for their predecessors, and that citizens can learn from the mistakes of their forebearers. In his speech commemorating the anniversary of the Tartu Peace Treaty on February 2, 2006, Estonian President Toomas Hendrik Ilves cautioned against the politicization of history in contemporary Estonia. The relocation of controversial monuments such as the Bronze Soldier cannot solve the integration problems in contemporary Estonia. The differences in Estonian and Russian understandings of recent history are related to contemporary Russian historiography and the lack of Estonian historian scholarship about twentieth-century Estonia. President Ilves's speech emphasized the importance of historical investigation of Estonian occupation that would not only examine the Estonian nation as a victim of communism, but also examine how collaboration and informing were integral parts of the Soviet regime in Estonia.

> The whole Soviet occupation in its entirety must be examined. Including the times we may not please, when the blame may not rest only on the shoulders of the occupiers from abroad. Collaborationism in Estonia is as little examined here as occupation has been in Russia. If we wish not to fall into the same trap of selective treatment history that we see to the East, we must make an honest and thorough examination of Estonian history up to August 1991. Investigating history and understanding the past, my dear compatriots, is much more important and painstaking work than fighting with monuments. This is a job, moreover, that no one else will do for us. (Ilves 2007)[2]

---

2 Ilves's speech as President has certain echoes with President von Weizsäcker's famous speech in Berlin commemorating the fiftieth anniversary of the end of World War II on May 8, 1985. Both speeches rose above political rancor to emphasis the importance of historical analysis and public debate for the consolidation of democratic values. Both cautioned against using history as a tool for short-term political gain. The major difference between the two speeches was that while Weizsäcker's speech was widely received in West Germany and abroad, very little attention was paid to the substance of Ilves' speech.

One important way in which to avoid labeling Russian-speakers living in the Baltics as collectively guilty for the crimes of communism is to separate the actions of a criminal regime from the people in whose name the crimes were done. As Ilves argued, Estonian politics focuses too much on group identity and not enough on individual citizens. While government bears responsibility for the previous regime, guilt is only individual not collective (Ilves 2008).

Respect and Plurality

If Mouffe (and Schmitt) envision politics as power and persuasion, Arendt imagines politics as the only space where freedom might occur. 'The answer to the question of the meaning of politics is so simple and so conclusive that one might think all other answers are utterly beside the point. The answer is: the meaning of politics is freedom' (Arendt 2005: 108). Particularly when individuals feel that their collective identity is at stake, conflicts over how different memories of the past are officially recognized by the state become more heated. If divisive issues are not discussed, but confined to the private sphere, they are avoided rather than addressed. In the case of conflicts involving public representations of the past in the form of monuments, museum exhibitions and history books—more public debate and political representation, rather than less is needed. Democracy as both a form of government and way of life is enriched by an understanding of citizenship that based more on *demos* than *ethnos*. Given the violent national excesses of the twentieth century and the demographic changes in Europe due to the ideological extremism of fascism and communism, defining 'the people' primarily by culture or blood has historically proven dubious and dangerously short-sighted. The challenge is to find points of common interest and understanding between individuals while still respecting cultural differences. One can only hope that belonging to a Europe that has learned from ideological extremism will be that common bridge between Balts and their Russian-speaking minorities. The hope is also that commemorative days such as May 9 can symbolize not only Victory Day from the Soviet-Russian side, but more importantly, a day for reflecting on a common European project of an open pluralist society which is more inclusive and postnational, rather than xenophobic and fixated on eternal antagonism.

References

Arendt, H. 1958. *The Human Condition*. Chicago, IL: University of Chicago Press.
Arendt, H. 1982. *Lectures on Kant's Political Philosophy*. Chicago, IL: University of Chicago Press.
Arendt, H. 2003. *Responsibility and Judgment*, edited by J. Kohn. New York: Schocken Books.

Arendt, H. 2005. *The Promise of Politics*, edited by J. Kohn. New York: Schocken Books.
Benhabib, S. 1990. Hannah Arendt and the Redemptive Power of Narrative. *Social Research*, 57:1, Spring, 167-196.
Berlin, I. 1998. My Intellectual Path, in *The Power of Ideas*. Princeton, NJ: Princeton University Press, 1-23.
Berlin, I. 2003. The Pursuit of the Ideal, in *The Crooked Timber of Humanity: Chapters in the History of Ideas*. London: Pimlico, 1-19.
Dahrendorf, R. 1990. *Reflections on the Revolution in Europe*. New York: Times Books.
Herder, J.G. 1993. *Against Pure Reason: Writings on Religion, Language and History*, trans. Marcia Bunge. Minneapolis, MN: Ausburg Fortress Press.
Ilves, T.H. 2007. Eesti ei kirjuta oma ajalugu ümber. *Eesti Päevaleht*, February 3.
Ilves, T.H. 2008. Speech at the presidential conference 'Erinevad mälud – ühine ulevik' [Different memories – common future], November 21, 2008, available at: http://www.president.ee/print.me.php?gid=122202. Accessed December 12, 2008.
Judt, T. 2002. The Past is another Country: Myth and Memory in Postwar Europe, in *Memory and Power in Post-War Europe*, edited by J-W. Müller. Cambridge: Cambridge University Press, 157-183.
Lagerspetz, M. 1999. Postsocialism as a Return: Notes on a Discursive Strategy. *East European Politics and Societies*, 13:2, Spring, 377-390.
Margalit, A. 2002. *The Ethics of Memory*. Cambridge, MA: Harvard University Press.
Misztal, B.A. 2004. The Sacralization of Memory. *European Journal of Social Theory*, 7:1, 67-84.
Misztal, B.A. 2005. Memory and Democracy. *American Behavioral Scientist* 48:10, June, 1320-1338.
Mouffe, C. 2000. *The Democratic Paradox*. London: Verso.
Mouffe, C. 2002. Politics and Passions: The Stakes of Democracy. *CSC Perspectives Working Papers*. Available at: http://www.wmin.ac.uk/sshl/page-221. Accessed April 22, 2009.
Mouffe, C. 2005 (1992). *The Return of the Political*. London: Verso.
Mouffe C. 2007. Artistic Activism and Agonistic Politics. *Art and Research: A Journal of Ideas, Contexts and Methods*, 1:2, Summer, 1-5.
Oathwaite, W. and Ray, L. 2005. Modernity, Memory and Postcommunism in *Social Theory and Postcommunism*. London: Blackwell, 176-196.
Popper, K. 1966 (1945). *The Open Society and its Enemies*. Vol. 1 and 2. London: Routledge.
Rorty, R. 1989. *Contingency, Irony and Solidarity*. Cambridge: Cambridge University Press.
Santayana, G. 1998. *The Life of Reason*. Amherst: Prometheus Books.
Schaap, A. 2007. Political Theory and the Agony of Politics. *Political Studies Review*, 5, 56-74.

Schmitt, C. 1979 (1932). *The Concept of the Political*, trans. G. Schwab. Chicago, IL: University of Chicago Press.
The Economist. 2007. The Rewriting of History. November 8.
Vico, G. 1948. *The New Science of Giambattista Vico*, trans. T.G. Bergin and M.H. Fisch. Ithaca, NY: Cornell University Press.

Chapter 8
The Fata Morgana of Revolution

From our vantage point in the 21st century, twenty odd years after the East European revolutions of 1989, the moment of collective action and solidarity seems to have taken place long ago, in an another country or time. Inserted into school textbooks, museum exhibits, coffee table history books and academic scholarship, 1989 has joined the rich lineage and chronicle of revolutions. It has become a singular event crystallized around a number, frozen into a date. As one of the important dates associated with key historical events, 1989 joins that of 1776, 1789 and 1917. Symbolizing radical newness and rupture, revolutions represent the pinnacle of political action. They embody the hopes of ordinary people into a kind of magical solidarity of concerted action and freedom. Following in the footsteps of Edmund Burke's *Reflections on the Revolution in France* and Karl Marx's *Eighteenth Brumaire*, Hannah Arendt is one of the most original thinkers to have reflected on the relation between revolution, freedom and political action in the twentieth century. As one who presents a philosophy of natality, new beginnings and action, Arendt's thinking has been linked with that of Martin Heidegger and St. Augustine. It is, however in her historical reflections on the lost treasure of the revolutionary spirit that she is perhaps closer to Walter Benjamin. When Arendt and her husband, Heinrich Blücher immigrated to the United States in 1941, she carried with her some manuscripts that Benjamin had given to her in Marseille in 1940, among them his 'Theses on the Philosophy of History.' Benjamin tried to cross the Pyrenees with an earlier group; however when the Spanish authorities closed the border, he despaired and took his life. A few months later, Arendt and Blücher successfully made the same journey from France into Spain. Once they arrived in New York, Arendt gave Benjamin's manuscripts to Theodor Adorno and his 'Theses' were published first in German and then later, in *Illuminations*, edited by Arendt herself. As recent scholarship has shown, many of the ways that Arendt describes Walter Benjamin resonate with her own political thought (Benhabib 2000, de Valk 2010, Marchart 2006). Referring to him as a pearl diver, who could recover forgotten treasures from the sea, she reflects on a passage from *The Tempest*.

> Full fathom five thy father lies,
> Of his bones are coral made,
> Those are pearls that were his eyes.
> Nothing of him that doth fade
> But doth suffer a sea-change
> Into something rich and strange.
> *The Tempest*, Act 1, Scene II

The poetic image of how the father's bones became coral and his eyes changed to pearls is a metaphor for how elements or fragments from the past undergo a sea-change when they are encountered in the present. Arendt characterized Benjamin as one who went to the bottom of the sea in search of beautiful treasures from the past. For her, his thinking was that of a pearl diver who rescued traces of tradition from the past and found new paths for thinking about history.

> Like a pearl diver who descends to the bottom of the sea, not to excavate the bottom and bring it to light but to pry loose the rich and the strange, the pearls and the coral in the depths, and to carry them to the surface, this thinking delves into the depths of the past – but not in order to resuscitate it the way it was and to contribute to the renewal of extinct ages. What guides this thinking is the conviction that although the living is subject to the ruin of time, the process of decay is at the same time a process of crystallization, that in the depth of the sea, into which sinks and is dissolved what once was alive, some things 'suffer a sea-change' and survive in new crystallized forms and shapes that remain immune to the elements, as though they waited only for the pearl diver who one day will come down to them and bring them up into the world of the living – as 'thought fragments,' as something 'rich and strange,' and perhaps even as everlasting *Urphänomene*. (Arendt 1968: 50-51)

What Arendt finds so fascinating in Benjamin's essays and literary criticism is precisely the fact that 'the process of decay is at the same time a process of crystallization.' In thinking about beginnings, revolution, action, freedom and politics, she excavates the meanings of concepts that capture the experience of the political. One can trace four points where Arendt, as a kind of pearl diver illuminates the process of decay and crystallization of the revolutionary treasure: the memory of revolution as an event outside of ordinary time; revolution as a fleeting fata morgana; the dangers of the absolute in politics and the nature of revolutionary time.

Remembering the Event of Revolution

In *On Revolution* and *Between Past and Future*, Arendt reflects on the nature of the political both in ordinary and extraordinary moments. The revolutionary spirit that she brings forth from the United States in 1776, France in 1789 and Hungary in 1956 was a treasure or moment infused with extraordinary meaning, outside of ordinary time. Similar to Benjamin, Arendt's thinking illuminates the process of decay and crystallization of the revolutionary treasure, as something both 'rich and strange.' In many ways, one could argue that Arendt is concerned less with what happened during the revolutionary moment of 1776, 1789, 1956, and I would say, by extension 1989. Rather she is more interested in how the event of those revolutions has been remembered and become an exemplary model for future action. As she herself writes, 'If there was a single *event* (*sic*) that shattered the bond between the New World and the countries of the old Continent, it was the French Revolution, which, in the view of its contemporaries, might never have come to pass without the glorious example on the other side of the Atlantic' (Arendt 1963: 215). Revolutions are events that may or may not be accompanied by violence. Arendt's prescient reflections on revolution bring into sharper focus the unpredictable ways that memories of revolution may affect political action in the present and future.

> If we want to learn what a revolution is – its general implications for man as a political being, its political significance for the world we live in, its role in modern history – we must turn to those historical moments when revolution made its appearance, assumed a kind of definite shape, and began to cast its spell over the minds of men, quite independent of the abuses and cruelties and deprivation of liberty which might have caused them to rebel. (Ibid: 43-44)

Arendt seeks to illuminate how revolution, as a modern political concept, associated with freedom and concerted action 'began to cast its spell over the mind of men.' It is precisely this magical kind of 'spell' that accompanies the memory of revolution that Arendt excavates. George Kateb aptly captures the importance of political action as exemplary and memorable. 'Put simply, Arendt thinks that political action has to be something memorable. It exists to be memorable, to become the stuff of stories immediately after it is done, and the stuff of history in later generations' (Kateb 2000: 133). If, in her more philosophical writings, Arendt interprets natality as an existential kind of newness, origin and beginning, it is in *On Revolution* that she focuses on new beginnings as the institutional and constitutional foundation of the republic, as well as revolutions as exemplary models of political action (Kalyvas 2008). She balances discussion of collective and juridical acts of political foundation with existential moments of authenticity that actors experienced when they participated in the French and American revolutions. What Arendt found deeply troubling though in revolutions was their dangerous tendency to regress into violence. Violence is not a necessary precondition for revolution, but tends historically to accompany the revolutionary foundation of a new polity.

In her discussion and comparison of the French and American revolutions, she examines how the revolutionary spirit has changed as it is brought forward from the past into the present. Hers is not only a hermeneutical interpretation of the past from the perspective of the present, but is similar to the rescuing critique that she most admired in Benjamin. 'Walter Benjamin knew that the break in tradition and the loss of authority which occurred in his lifetime were irreparable, and he concluded that he had to discover new ways of dealing with the past' (Arendt 1968: 38). The same sentiment could be said of Arendt as well. The loss of German citizenship, sense of belonging, fractured identity as pariah or parvenu, German or Jew, indeed the loss of the world of European Jewry could never be regained. Nonetheless, Arendt like Benjamin sought 'new ways of dealing with the past'—new ways to overcome the dulling encroachment of the social realm and the desert of totalitarian ideologies. In thinking about tradition, she also acts as a pearl diver who unearths treasures, fragments and ciphers from the past that illuminate the present—even if, only for a moment. Treasures from the past contain a certain truth. In an interesting passage, she likens Benjamin to Heidegger and his conception of truth as *aletheia* or unconcealment (*Unverborgenheit*).

> Without realizing it, Benjamin actually had more in common with Heidegger's remarkable sense for living eyes and living bones that had sea-changed into pearls and coral, and as such could be saved and lifted into the present only be doing violence to their context in interpreting them with "the deadly impact" of new thoughts, than he did with the dialectical subtleties of his Marxist friends. (Ibid., 46)

Just as Benjamin found his way back to the past through collections and quotations that on the surface appear chaotic, so Arendt herself engages in overlapping reflections on the tradition of political thought and philosophy—in the hope of recovering treasures that may illuminate the darkness of the present. She saw a correspondence or elective affinity between the artistic and political desire to find a link to the past. Like Heidegger, she is attentive to the words themselves and to the different meanings that a single word contains.

> Any period to which its own past has become questionable as it has to us must eventually come up against the phenomenon of language, for in it the past is contained ineradicably, thwarting all attempts to get rid of it once and for all. The Greek *polis* will continue to exist at the bottom of our political existence – that is, at the bottom of the sea – for as long as we use the world "politics." (Ibid., 49)

The Fata Morgana of the Revolutionary Tradition

Arendt's mediations on revolution are linked to her earlier reflections on totalitarianism. If totalitarianism was a new political phenomenon that crystallized the elements of anti-Semitism, imperialism and totalitarianism by aiming to eradicate the modern individual, the revolutionary spirit offers hope for change and collective action. 'Totalitarian domination, like tyranny, bears the germs of its own destruction' (Arendt 1973: 478). The source of Arendt's hope is the simple fact that each person is unique and a beginning. Contingency, spontaneity and creativity are part of human life. In her preface to *Between Past and Future*, she reflects on the tragic loss of the revolutionary spirit in the French Resistance, 1776, 1789 and 1956.

> The men of the European Resistance were neither the first nor the last to lose their treasure. The history of revolutions – from the summer of 1776 in Philadelphia and the summer of 1789 in Paris to the autumn of 1956 in Budapest – which politically spells out the innermost story of the modern age, could be told in parable form as the tale of an age-old treasure which, under the most varied circumstances, appears abruptly, unexpectedly, and disappears again, under different mysterious circumstances, as though it were a fata morgana. (Arendt 1993: 4-5)

By placing the history of revolutions as 'the innermost story of the modern age,' Arendt links the memory of revolution with modernity. As Seyla Benhabib argues, Arendt's historiography from *On Totalitarianism* onwards is linked to that of Benjamin. Given the break in tradition and emergence of totalitarianism, she argues that Arendt developed 'a conception of political theory as "storytelling"' (Benhabib 2000: 87). Similar to Benjamin's pearl diver, who uncovers fragments from the past in order to illuminate the present, Arendt foregrounds storytelling and narrative. It is the nature of a revolution to be short-lived. The revolutionary moment cannot last, but is fleeting and fades into ordinary empty time. Each attempt to capture a revolution is like trying to grasp a fata morgana—an optical illusion or mirage that one can see faintly on the horizon. Arendt admires revolutions for being foundational and for beginning something new. '[R]evolutions are the only political events which confront us directly and inevitably with the problem of beginning' (Arendt 1963: 21). In destroying the past political order, revolutions claim to begin *ex nihilo*, to wipe the slate clean so that one begins from nothing— and yet, the people and the places in the body politic remain the same. 'Crucial, then, to any understanding of revolutions in the modern age is that the idea of freedom and the experience of a new beginning should coincide' (Ibid., 29). Even if some revolutions end in violent failure, the revolutionary moment of collective action, concerted freedom and radical change depict the brief time when freedom and a new beginning co-existed.

The revolutionary moment is neither one of blind optimism nor a Hegelian grand narrative culminating in freedom and progress. Rather, the revolutionary treasure contains an 'enormous pathos' (Ibid., 34). Fascinated by the revolutionary attempt to house freedom through the constitutional act of foundation, Arendt recognizes its ephemeral and transitory nature. The revolutionary treasure is a fata morgana, a beautiful and mysterious mirage that lives for a very brief time. At the core of the revolutionary spirit is the *promise* of a better world. Here, although one might be tempted to ask whether this fata morgana is really a seductive siren offering the utopian promise of heavenly perfection, its very transitory quality denies any permanence. 'Only where this pathos of novelty is present and where novelty is connected with the idea of freedom are we entitled to speak of revolution' (Ibid.).

Political beginnings likewise contain the principle of beginning in the sense of constitutional foundation. But revolutionary beginnings are fraught with the paradox of trying to found something permanent. Because the foundation of a new state is the aim of revolution, it necessarily means the end of that self-same revolution. 'From which it unfortunately seems to follow that nothing threatens the very achievements of revolution more dangerously and more acutely than the spirit which has brought them about' (Ibid., 232). If *The Origins of Totalitarianism* outlines a tragic view of twentieth century Europe, *On Revolution* looks to moments in history where freedom and hope crystallized in the experience of the French and American revolutions. The *pathos* of the revolutionary spirit is already present in the very act of political foundation. Recalling the violent origins of Judeo-Christianity with the story of Cain and Abel and the foundation of Rome with Romulus' killing of his brother, Remus—Arendt links political foundation with violent crime. 'The tale spoke clearly: whatever brotherhood human beings may be capable of has grown out of fratricide, whatever political organization men may have achieved has its origin in crime' (Ibid., 20). Violence and fratricide are not only the antecedents to modern revolution, but were present both in the terror following the French Revolution and in the violence of slavery in the United States during and after the American Revolution. Here one might also draw a parallel with Benjamin's famous reflection on the thin line dividing civilization from violent barbarism. 'There is no document of civilization which is not at the same time a document of barbarism. And just as such a document is not free of barbarism, barbarism taints also the manner in which it was transmitted from one owner to another' (Benjamin 1968: 256).

The transformation of the meaning of revolution from the scientific to political world is more than semantic. If revolution originally signified the cyclical movement of the planets, its first political use meant the restoration of monarchial power during the Glorious Revolution of 1688. 'The fact that the word 'revolution' meant originally restoration, hence something which to us is its very opposite, is not a mere oddity of semantics' (Arendt 1963: 43). It was only in the eighteenth century that political revolution was associated with a new beginning. In a famous conversation during the storming of the Bastille on July 14, 1789, King Louis XVI remarked to his messenger, 'C'est une révolte.' He was then corrected, 'Non, Sire, c'est une révolution' (Ibid., 47). If a revolt is an upheaval soon to be quashed, a revolution unleashes an unpredictable and spontaneous power. 'The emphasis has entirely shifted from the lawfulness of a rotating, cyclical movement to its irresistibility' (Ibid., 47-48). It is precisely this notion of 'irresistibility' and of the desire for freedom conceptualized alongside historical necessity that distinguished the violence of the French Revolution from the foundational moment of freedom in the American experience. For Arendt, the important point is to disentangle freedom from liberation. 'The difficulty here is that revolution as we know it in the modern age has been concerned with both liberation and freedom' (Ibid., 32). She characterizes the French Revolution as one of liberation from poverty while the American Revolution embodies the housing of freedom through the constitutional limit of state power. While it is impossible to relive the revolutionary moments because the event of revolution is a fata morgana, one can catch a glimpse of that experience. 'The revolutionary spirit of the last centuries, that is the eagerness to liberate *and* to build a new house where freedom can dwell, is unprecedented and unequalled in all prior history' (Ibid., 35) If the French Revolution was rooted in a notion of public freedom and the primacy of the social question, the American Revolution was preoccupied with public happiness and the foundation of freedom. Although the French Revolution is remembered as *the* model of political revolutions, Arendt highlights important elements from the American experience that are relevant to the East European revolutions of 1989; namely the emphasis on individual freedom over equality and the desire to limit and contain power.

The Dangers of the Absolute in Politics

Revolutions should not be equated with violent regime change; instead they embody the brief appearance of freedom and constitutional foundation. In an effort to understand politics and action and to distinguish revolution from violence, Arendt resists equating power, strength, force and authority as synonyms. 'Indeed one of the most obvious distinctions between power and violence is that power always stands in need of numbers, whereas violence up to a point can without them because it relies on implements' (Arendt 1969: 140-141) Power is intersubjective and lies in the space between people. 'Power corresponds to the human ability not just to act but to act in concert. Power is never the property of an individual; it belongs to a group and remains in existence only so long as the group keeps together' (Ibid., 143). As soon as the group dissipates, power vanishes. Strength, on the other hand designates something inherent in a person. Force, which is often used as a synonym for violence indicates 'energy released by physical or social movements' (Ibid., 144). Authority is a term that Arendt sees more in those who obey. 'Its hallmark is unquestioning recognition by those who are asked to obey; neither coercion nor persuasion is needed' (Ibid., 144). Unlike power, which is *between* people, violence is distinguished by its instrumental character over another person. 'Power springs up whenever people get together and act in concert, but it derives its legitimacy from the initial getting together rather than from any action that then may follow' (Ibid., 151). It is this initial event in revolutions, this act of political beginning and foundation that is remembered and commemorated that fascinates Arendt. 'The initial getting together' and moments of solidarity constitute the enormous power of the political. In the end, Arendt argues 'power and violence are opposites; where the one rules absolutely, the other is absent' (Ibid., 155).

One of the most far-reaching consequences of the French Revolution was 'the birth of the modern concept of history and Hegel's philosophy' (Arendt 1963: 51). For her, the revolutionary spirit crystallized in the philosophy of Hegel and Marx. The very images of movement and glorious deeds transformed moments of freedom into ones of historical necessity.

> Yet the point of the matter is that all those who, throughout the nineteenth century and deep into the twentieth, followed in the footsteps of the French Revolution saw themselves not merely as successes of the men of the French Revolution but as agents of history and historical necessity, with the obvious and yet paradoxical result that instead of freedom necessity became the chief political category of political and revolutionary thought. (Ibid., 52-53)

Here one might say that the transformation or sea-change of freedom into historical necessity also signaled the decay of the revolutionary treasure. The reduction of human spontaneous action into necessity and spectacle deformed freedom into necessity. In her story of the tragic failure of the French Revolution, Arendt traces how the social question and the desire to eliminate poverty missed the moment when freedom could be founded. Recalling Melville's *Billy Budd* and Dostoevsky's *The Grand Inquisitor*, Arendt warns against introducing the Absolute into human affairs. The French Revolution reversed the primordial criminal origins of political life. Afterwards, it is no longer Cain (the guilty evil one) who slew Abel (the innocent), but Abel (in the guise of the innocent French masses) who slew Cain (the corrupt French monarchy). 'The absolute – and to Melville an absolute was incorporated with the Rights of Man – spells doom to everyone when it is introduced into the political realm' (Ibid., 84). By equating the desire for freedom with liberation from poverty and seeking to channel the spontaneous energy of revolution into a narrative of historical necessity, the motif of history became an Absolute in which revolutionary actors became spectators carried along in a drama that they could no longer control. The beheading of King Louis XVI symbolized the severing of the head from the French political body and marked the violent origin of a new political beginning.

Although Arendt, the pearl diver wants to retrieve positive moments from both the French and American Revolutions, she is more critical of the French Revolution for its violent privileging of equality over freedom and the primacy of the social over that of the political. Each founding moment of freedom or *constitution libertatis*, however encounters the problem of the Absolute. In her opinion, the American Revolution was miraculously saved from the belief that power and law sprang from the same source because the federal constitution derived its authority from the 13 colonies and, from the town halls within each of those colonies. If power was constituted and limited from below in the American Revolutionary experience, the French Revolution kept power in the hands of the revolutionary momentum *itself*. The problem of the Absolute occurs at the very moment of the foundation of a polity. It occurs with the paradoxical source of man-made laws. 'It is the very nature of a beginning to carry with itself a measure of complete arbitrariness' (Ibid., 206). From where does the law derive its authority: from tradition, the present generation or from God? For Arendt, the revolutionary moment occurs as a hiatus or gap between past and future. Unlike Carl Schmitt, she locates authority in the revolutionary experience of freedom, not in the exception of the sovereign. Cautious of ever introducing the Absolute into politics whether embodied as the General Will, the Sovereign or the people, she maintains the primacy of plurality, freedom and spontaneity. 'The hope for man in his singularity lay in the fact that not man but men inhabit the earth and form a world between them. It is human worldliness that will save men from the pitfalls of human nature' (Ibid., 175).

If the French Revolution derived power from the revolution momentum and the general will of the people, the American Revolution envisioned power in covenants and promises between people. 'There is an element of the world-building capacity of man in the human faculty of making and keeping promises' (Ibid., 175). It was precisely this ability to make and keep promises that Arendt sought to rescue in her retelling of the story of revolutions. What Arendt found fascinating and worth cultivating in the American experience was that the revolution was one of political rather than social foundation. 'The problem they posed was not social but political, it concerned not the order of society but the form of government' (Ibid., 68). In all fairness and particularly from the vantage point of hindsight, one might say also that it was the tragic misfortune of the American Founding Fathers not to pay more attention to the social inequalities both in slavery and towards Native Americans in the founding of the Republic. Arendt does not write about the legacy of violence against Native Americans and only briefly alludes to slavery. When she does, her comments are prescient. 'It is as though the American Revolution was achieved in a kind of ivory tower into which the fearful spectacle of human misery, the haunting voices of abject poverty, never penetrated' (Ibid., 95). Both slavery and the violence towards Native Americans were, however important and violent chapters in American history and confirm Arendt's original intuition that political foundation is often founded on fratricide. In comparing the French and American revolutions, she reflects on the violent potential of pity. 'Pity may be the perversion of compassion, but its alternative is solidarity' (Ibid., 88). In absolute form, pity has more potential for violence than solidarity. In a sense, the French Revolution made pity into an absolute, while the Americans focused on freedom and ignored social inequalities. 'From this, we can only conclude that the institution of slavery carries an obscurity even blacker than the obscurity of poverty; the slave, not the poor man, was "wholly overlooked"' (Ibid., 71).

The Revolutionary Time of *Nunc Stans* and *Jetztzeit*

One crucial aspect of revolutions is their different sense of time. Revolutions entail the consciousness of a new sense of time or a new secular order: *Novus Ordo Seclorum*. The revolutionary moment is extraordinary and stands outside of ordinary temporality. Both Benjamin and Arendt were fascinated by the fleeting temporality of the present. Inspired by Augustine, Arendt understood the present to be a temporal gap or space in between a past that is no longer and a future that is not yet. Time has a capricious and paradoxical quality to it.

> This small non-time-space in the very heart of time, unlike the world and the culture into which we are born, can only be indicated, but cannot be inherited and handed down from the past; each new generation, indeed every human being as he inserts himself between an infinite past and an infinite future, must discover and ploddingly pave it anew. (Arendt 1993: 13)

In an interesting footnote to the English translation of Benjamin's 'Theses' that she herself edited, Arendt calls attention to the similarity between his *Jetztzeit* and the *nunc stans* as the gap between past and future. 'Benjamin says "*Jetztzeit*" and indicates by the quotation marks that he does not simply mean an equivalent to *Gegenwart*, that is, present. He clearly is thinking of the mystical *nunc stans*' (Arendt's footnote in Benjamin 1968: 261). *Jetztzeit* or now-time for Benjamin is mystical and full of meaning. 'History is the subject of a structure whose site is not homogeneous, empty time, but time filled by, the presence of the now (*Jetztzeit*)' (Benjamin 1968: 261). Reflecting on the French Revolution, Benjamin indicates the awareness of Robespierre for ancient Rome. 'Thus, to Robespierre ancient Rome was a past charged with the time of the now which he blasted out of the continuum of history' (Ibid.). If Benjamin's mystical sense of the present or *Jetztzeit* is filled with the redemptive expectation of the Messiah, Arendt's *nunc stans* is more worldly. She does not look towards an angel or God for redemption, but to the creative potential within human beings themselves. Where she might be characterized as mystical is in her depiction of the miracle of human action. 'Our whole existence rests, after all, on a chain of miracles, as it were...' (Arendt 1993: 169) The miraculous is very much part of our existence. While Benjamin looks outside the world for moments of revolutionary change, Arendt remains firmly within the world. We should not wait for the spectacular coming of the Messiah, but look within the world of human action.

> History, in contradistinction to nature, is full of events; here the miracle of accident and infinite probability occurs so frequently that it seems strange to speak of miracles at all. But the reason for this frequency is merely that historical processes are created and constantly interrupted by human initiative, by the *initium* man is insofar as he is an acting being. Hence it is not in the least superstitious, it is even a counsel of realism, to look for the unforeseeable and unpredictable, to be prepared for and to expect 'miracles' in the political realm. (Ibid., 170)

If the gaze of Benjamin's melancholic angel of history is turned towards the past while physically moving towards the future, Arendt's gaze is focused on the present. 'The temporal dimension of the *nunc stans* experience in the activity of thinking gathers the absent tenses, the not-yet and the no-more, together into its own presence' (Arendt 1978: 211). There is not a single metaphor for an angelic figure or Messiah, but the open space within one's own mind and in between people. Perhaps the polis for her is the lost treasure *par excellence*. 'But the loss of worldly permanence and reliability – which politically is identified with the loss of authority – does not entail, at least not necessarily, the loss of the human capacity for building, preserving, and caring for a world that can survive us and remain a place fit to live in for those who come after us' (Arendt 1993: 95). It is precisely Arendt's hope in the human capacity for building, caring and preserving the world that she rescues from the American experience. The human ability to make covenants with one another and to make promises for the future is captured in the revolutionary moment of 1776. In reflecting on the French and American Revolutions, Arendt reminds us of the extraordinary power of promising to found a different and better society in the future. Although promises and covenants are inherent in the idea of a social contract, she traces the idea of political and existential origins to St. Augustine. Man is always a beginner—full of spontaneity, creativity and contingency. For Arendt, revolutions are the embodiment of political beginnings.

> What matters in our context is less the profoundly Roman notion that all foundations are re-establishments and reconstructions than the somehow connected but different idea that men are equipped for the logically paradoxical task of making a new beginning because they themselves are new beginnings and hence beginners, that the very capacity for beginning is rooted in natality, in the fact that human beings appear in the world by virtue of birth. (Arendt 1963: 211)

Unlike Benjamin's understanding of the now or *Jetztzeit*, which is rooted in Jewish Mysticism, Arendt's *nunc stans* is influenced by Augustine's reflections on time. Time began with man and not before. Recalling Augustine, Arendt emphasizes the fact that man is a beginner. 'The purpose of the creation of man was to make possible a beginning: "That there be a beginning man was created, before whom nobody was."' (Arendt 1978: 217) The gap between past and future is the space where man inserts himself into the world. The *nunc stans* is a moment both of the possibility for action and thinking. 'The gap, though we hear about it first as a *nunc stans*, the "standing now" in medieval philosophy, where it served, in the form of *nunc aeternitatis*, as model and metaphor for divine eternity, is not a historical datum; it seems to be coeval with the existence of man on earth' (Ibid., 210). Interestingly enough in her last book, *The Life of the Mind*, Arendt again reflects on the same quotation from *The Tempest* that she referred to with respect to Benjamin. Only now, she calls attention to herself as a kind of pearl diver retrieving lost treasures from the past.

> What has been lost is the continuity of the past as it seemed to be handed down from generation to generation, developing in the process its own consistency. The dismantling process has its own technique, and I did not go into that here except peripherally. What you then are left with is still the past, but a *fragmented* past, which has lost its certainty of evaluation… It is with such fragments from the past, after their sea-change, that I have dealt here. (Arendt 1978: 212)

Arendt's emphasis on a 'fragmented past, which has lost its certainty of evaluation' rings true today, twenty years after the East European revolutions. The gap between the revolutionary spirit of 1989 and some of the disappointing rancor of post-communist politics couldn't be sharper. Particularly in today's media age, where images of East European citizens protesting in national capitals are frozen as modern day icons in film and photography, the memory of 1989 is one of collective solidarity, the desire for freedom and hope in the future. Often times the memory of those revolutions, as one of nonviolent solidarity against communism and for freedom is buried beneath the more pressing problems of social fragmentation, minority issues and political apathy. Revolutions are the extraordinary culmination and embodiment of political action. Indeed, as Stefan Auer writes with respect to Arendt: 'Revolutions are those magic moments in human history that showed that men and women, when acting in concert, were able to transcend the limits of their biological existence and pursue ideals of freedom' (Auer 2006).

For Arendt, there is an art to telling a story. In the narrative, certain individuals are heroic and become exemplary models for later generations. Arendt's fondness for heroic deeds extends from Homer to Shakespeare, and to some of the founding fathers of the American Revolution. If there is a moral in Arendt's marvelous tale of revolution that she rescues from the depth of the sea, it is one of pathos, unpredictability, heroism, contingency and the miracle of human action. 'If these legends could teach anything at all, their lessons indicated that freedom is no more the automatic result of liberation then the new beginning is the automatic consequence of the end' (Arendt 1963: 205). The event of revolutions expresses the highest potential that individuals have for collective action; however once that moment passes, it becomes a fata morgana that is impossible to wholly grasp. It becomes a beautiful mirage captured in memory, retold in narrative and crystallized into a date outside of ordinary time.

References

Arendt, H. 1963. *On Revolution.* New York: Penguin Books.
Arendt, H. 1968. Introduction. Walter Benjamin 1892-1940, in *Illuminations* by Walter Benjamin, New York: Schocken Books, 1-55.
Arendt, H. 1969. *Crises of the Republic.* New York: Harcourt Brace Jovanovich, 103-198.
Arendt, H. 1973 (1951). *The Origins of Totalitarianism.* New York: Harcourt Brace Jovanovich.
Arendt, H. 1978. *The Life of the Mind.* New York: Harcourt Brace Jovanovich.
Arendt, H. 1993 (1954). *Between Past and Future: Eight Exercises in Political Thought.* New York: Penguin Books.
Auer, S. 2006. The Lost Treasure of the Revolution. Originally published in *Osteuropa*, 9. Available at www.eurozine.com. Accessed November 19, 2010.

Benhabib, S. 2000. *The Reluctant Modernism of Hannah Arendt*. Lanham, MD: Rowman & Littlefield Publishers.

Benjamin, W. 1968. Theses on the Philosophy of History, in *Illuminations*, trans. Harry Zohn. New York, Schocken Books, 253-267.

de Valk, E. 2010. The Pearl Divers. Hannah Arendt, Walter Benjamin and the Demands of History. *Krise: Journal for Contemporary Philosophy*, Issue 1. Available at http://www.krisis.eu/content/2010-1/krisis-2010-1-04-devalk.pdf. Accessed November 12, 2010.

Kalyvas, A. 2008. *Democracy and the Politics of the Extraordinary. Max Weber, Carl Schmitt and Hannah Arendt*. Cambridge: Cambridge University Press.

Kateb, G. 2000. Political Action: Its Nature and Advantages, in *The Cambridge Companion to Hannah Arendt*, edited by Dana Villa. Cambridge: Cambridge University Press, 130-148.

Marchart, O. 2006. Time for a New Beginning. Arendt, Benjamin, and the Messianic Conception of Political Temporality. *Redescriptions: Yearbook of Political Thought and Conceptual History*, 134-147.

Shakespeare, W. 1987. *The Tempest*. Oxford: Oxford University Press.

Postscript
Europe between Past and Future

The fact that the twentieth anniversary of German unification on October 3rd passed by with little attention (outside of Germany) is a quiet reminder of just how much Europe has changed from 1945, or from 1990 for that matter. Likewise, the fact that Estonia adopted the euro in January 2011 with little fanfare (outside of Estonia) is another reminder of a silent sea change in Europe. The bitterly divided continent has become remarkably normal. In taking stock of the short twentieth century, the contrast between Europe's totalitarian past and democratic present is nothing short of a miracle. The past persists as a legacy shifting between an inheritance from previous generations and a traumatic burden to be carried by the next. The totalitarian past of Europe casts its shadow on the present in the sense that it is more than an ugly reminder of the dark side of modernity. It is also a singularly important chapter in modern European history. Zygmunt Bauman argues that categorical murder is not only one of the hallmarks of the twentieth century, but a deeply European phenomenon. 'Auschwitz and Kolyma were laboratories in which the limits of human pliability were researched, and most important, the most effective means of cleansing society of its disorderly, uncertainty-generating contaminations were experimented with and put to practical tests' (Bauman 2008: 85-86). Since pristine memory of the past is impossible, memory is subject to interpretation and prone to distortion, whether as a sacred event frozen outside of time or trivialized in stereotypes and clichés. As Bauman writes, 'memory is a *mixed* blessing' (Ibid., 91). Similar to Tzvetan Todorov and Timothy Garton Ash, Bauman is wary of casting Europe's totalitarian past as a sacred memory impervious to criticism. If the totalitarian thesis equates communism and Nazism as 'peas in pod,' their uniqueness as regime types is rather one of 'apples and oranges' (Todorov 2003: 74-90). Communism and Nazism were indeed similar, but not the same.

Claus Leggewie compares Europe's past to a battlefield with seven concentric circles. While the first six circles of twentieth century Europe were filled with the Holocaust, communism, expulsion, the Armenian question, European periphery and Europe as a migration continent, the seventh circle is represented by European renewal. If each circle is a battlefield between friend and enemy, the seventh denotes a common European heritage. Likewise, if the six circles interpret the past as a traumatic burden, the seventh envisions the European 'success story' as an inheritance. As Leggewie writes,

> Let us summarize: Europe's collective memory after 1989 is as multifaceted as its nations and cultures, and is divided, just as its national and social environments

> are. Memory cannot be mnemotechnically regulated and decreed by official state festivities and routine commemorative rituals, like May 8 or January 27. But the path toward a shared remembering of ancestral crimes, and a concomitant careful extraction of lessons for contemporary European democracies, can be a fully European path. (Leggewie 2008: 230)

Although memories are as diverse as the people and nationalities of Europe, the common 'European path' is to learn from the past, so as not to repeat the same mistakes in the future. History thus has a both a didactic and moral role. The issue is perhaps less *whether* one should remember the past and rather one of *how* to internalize the lessons of the past for the future of Europe. For Tony Judt, the twentieth century is marked by mis-memories and a facile tendency to substitute commemoration for learning from the past. The twentieth century is not only as Hobsbawm coined it, 'the short twentieth century,' it is more worryingly, 'the forgotten twentieth century' (Judt 2008). Given the dearth of commemorations, museums and monuments—how can Judt possibly claim that the twentieth century has been forgotten?

> In our Manichaean enthusiasms we in the West made haste to dispense whenever possible with the economic, intellectual, and institutional baggage of the twentieth century and encouraged others to do likewise. The belief that *that* was then and *this* is now, that all we had to learn from the past was not to repeat it, embraced much more than just the defunct institutions of Cold War-era Communism and its Marxist ideological membrane. Not only did we fail to learn very much from the past – this would hardly have been remarkable. But we have become stridently insistent – in our economic calculations, our political practices, our international strategies, even our education priorities – that *the past has nothing of interest to teach us*. (Ibid., 2)

If the past is only remembered through the prism of suffering or national solidarity, the larger, and perhaps more universal problem of inhumanity and lack of toleration for those, who espouse different beliefs, is silently avoided. Judt is making an important point. It is easier to erect a monument and freeze an image of the past, then to acknowledge the complexity of historical events. 'The twentieth century is hardly behind us, but already its quarrels and its dogmas, its ideals and its fears are slipping into the obscurity of mis-memory' (Ibid.). A mis-memory is not a direct falsification of history, but more often an embellished Manichean one of friend vs. enemy or victim vs. perpetrator. 'The overwhelming majority of places of official twentieth-century memory are either avowedly nostalgio-triumphalist—praising famous men and celebrating famous victories—or else, and increasingly, opportunities for the acknowledgement and recollection of selective suffering' (Ibid., 3). In the spirit of Nietzsche, Judt is concerned with the disproportionate attention given to monumental and antiquarian history. Similar to Garton Ash, he also warns that commemoration cannot be a substitute for history. The proliferation of museums and monuments should not replace the critical analysis of historians. In the age of liquid modernity, the speed of information can provide a facile illusion of distancing oneself from the past—into *that* was then and *this* is now. The different ways in which the World War II and the Holocaust are understood between East and West Europe demonstrate the need for more historical research rather than less.

To think about contemporary Europe between past and future is to think along with Hannah Arendt about the gap between past and future. As she wrote poetically,

> The gap, I suspect, is not a modern phenomenon, it is perhaps not even a historical datum but is coeval with the existence of man on earth. It may well be the region of the spirit or, rather, the path paved by thinking, this small track of non-time which the activity of thought beats within the time-space of mortal men and into which the trains of thought, of remembrance and anticipation, save whatever they touch from the ruin of historical and biographical time. (Arendt 1993: 13)

What then could be learned from Europe's twentieth century totalitarian *and* revolutionary past? In an Arendtian sense, a deep appreciation for the plurality and freedom experienced during the East European revolutions of 1989 has to be coupled with memories of totalitarianism and the Holocaust. Understanding the past is more of a continual process than finished event. 'Understanding begins with birth and ends with death. To the extent that the rise of totalitarian governments is the central event of our world, to understand totalitarianism is not to condone anything, but to reconcile ourselves to a world in which such things are possible at all' (Arendt 1994: 308). Combining Aristotle's *phronesis* with Kant's judgment, Arendt argues for the need to try and see things from different perspectives. Translated as practical wisdom or prudence, *phronesis* is 'the insight of the political man' (Arendt 2005: 168). 'Such insight into a political issue means nothing other than the greatest possible overview of all the possible standpoints and viewpoints from which an issue can be seen and judged (Ibid.). Likewise, Kant's 'enlarged mentality' enables us to think from the perspective of the other person. The insight of listening to others who have different opinions lies at the heart of pluralism and entails a deep respect for the humanity within each person. The human capacity to imagine how others feel in conjunction with knowledge of past failures is central for Arendt. The ability to listen and learn from others can be cultivated or ignored.

> Imagination alone enables us to see things in their proper perspective, to be strong enough to put that which is too close at a certain distance so that we can see and understand it without bias and prejudice, to be generous enough to bridge abysses of remoteness until we can see and understand everything that is too far away from us as though it were our own affair. (Arendt 1994: 323)

Such openness to the opinion of others and empathy for others by virtue of their humanity is echoed in the work of Zygmunt Bauman. In response to the question of what can be learned from Europe's recent past, Bauman argues unequivocally for the imperative of hospitality. Totalitarian crimes make hospitality and respect for one's neighbor more salient than ever. 'Indeed if ethics is a work of reason, as Kant wished it to be, then hospitality is—must be, or must sooner or later become—the first rule of human conduct' (Bauman 2008: 227). The legacy of totalitarianism makes hospitality imperative for the future of Europe. Likewise, the recognition and acceptance of the Holocaust as a shared part of European history makes the Kantian project of cosmopolitanism and perpetual peace even more important than when he wrote *Perpetual Peace* in the eighteenth century. Kantian hospitality implies dignity and respect towards one another. Hospitality is not philanthropy but a right. 'In this context, hospitality means the right of the stranger not to be treated with hostility when he arrives on someone else's territory' (Kant 2009: 28-29). The stranger is not only a guest to be well received by his or her host, but first and foremost, a human being who, by virtue of his humanity has the right to be respected by others. The earth is a finite place where everyone has the right to belong. Moreover, as Kant poignantly points out—the earth is a globe of finite territory. 'Since the earth is a globe, they cannot disperse over an infinite area, but must necessarily tolerate one another's company' (Ibid., 29). If toleration is only understood in a very thin way, it can easily fall into the superiority of the majority over those 'others' who make up the minority. The thicker version of hospitality that Kant, Arendt and Bauman, argue for is based upon the fundamental dignity of the person. Kant's conception of hospitality is grounded in his understanding of humanity. 'Act in such away that you treat humanity, whether in your own person or in the person of another, always at the same time as an end and never simply as a means' (Kant 1981: 36). As a secular version of the commandment to love one's neighbor, Kant argues for the fundamental dignity of each human being. Likewise his plea for cosmopolitanism emphasizes the common humanity of individuals over their national, religious and ethnic differences. In agreement with Kant, Bauman writes: 'Accepting the precept of loving one's neighbor is the birth act of humanity' (Bauman 2008: 32-33). One important lesson that could be learned from Europe's recent past is the necessity to recognize human dignity and ground hospitality in both the institutional framework of government and in the everyday attitudes of individuals. Granted this is a tall and idealist order, but one that keeps alive the memory of those who were deemed less than human under National Socialism and communism.

In a similar vein, Gadamer also reflects on what we can learn from recent European history. In his essay, 'The Variety of Europe's Heritage and Future,' he emphasizes the many-layered legacy of European culture and history. Given the multiplicity of languages, cultures and religious worldviews in Europe, one is confronted with difference everyday. 'To live with the Other, live as the Other's Other, is the fundamental human task – on the most lowly and the most elevated levels alike ... Hence perhaps the particular advantage of Europe, which could and *had* (*sic*) to learn the art of living with others' (Gadamer quoted in Bauman 2008: 241).[1] As the living memory of communism and National Socialism fades and becomes history, this lesson of having to learn how to live with others is part of Europe's legacy. Indeed, in Gadamer's opinion, learning from one another is the unique 'task' of Europe. 'I mean, that it is the future of mankind in a large sense, for which we all have to learn from one another, which is for us, our European task (*Aufgabe*)' (Gadamer 1989: 31).[2] Internalizing the Kantian values of hospitality and humanity in light of their absence during much of the twentieth century is not simply a dream, but an imperative. Indeed, as Bauman reflects on Gadamer, he makes an important argument for the particularity of the task of Europe. 'When seen against the background of the conflict-ridden planet, Europe looks like a laboratory where the tools necessary for Kant's universal unification of humanity keeps being designed, and a workshop in which they keep being tested in action, though for the time being in the performance of less ambitious, smaller-scale jobs' (Bauman 2008: 242).

References

Arendt, H. 1963. *On Revolution.* New York: Penguin Books.
Arendt, H. 1968. Introduction. Walter Benjamin 1892-1940, in *Illuminations* by Walter Benjamin, New York: Schocken Books.
Arendt, H. 1973 (1951). *The Origins of Totalitarianism.* New York: Harcourt Brace Jovanovich.
Arendt, H. 1993 (1954). *Between Past and Future: Eight Exercises in Political Thought.* New York: Penguin Books.
Arendt, H. 1994. *Essays in Understanding 1930-1954.* New York: Harcourt Brace.
Arendt, H. 2005. *The Promise of Politics.* New York: Schocken Books.
Bauman, Z. 2008. *Does Ethics have a Chance in a World of Consumers?* Boston, MA: Harvard University Press.
Gadamer, H.G. 1989. Die Vielfalt Europas Erbe und Zukunft, in *Das Erbe Europas.* Frankfurt: Suhrkamp, 7-34.
Judt, T. 2005. *Postwar: A History of Europe since 1945.* New York: Penguin Press.
Judt, T. 2008. *Reappraisals: Reflections on the Forgotten Twentieth Century.* New York: Penguin Books.

---

1 For the original quotation, see 'Mit dem Anderen leben, als der Andere des Anderen leben, diese menschliche Grundaufgabe gilt im kleinsten wie im grosser Massstab...Hier mag es ein besonderer Vorzug Europas sein, dass es mehr als andere Länder hat lernen können und hat lernen müssen, mit anderen zu leben, auch wenn die anderen anders sind' (Gadamer 1989: 30).

2 'Ich meine, dass es die Zukunft der Menschheit im ganzen sein wird, für die wir das alle miteinander zu erlernen haben, was unsere europäische Aufgabe für uns ist' (Gadamer 1989: 31).

Kant, I. 1981 (1785). *Grounding for the Metaphysics of Morals*, trans. James W. Ellington, Indianapolis, IN: Hackett Publishing Company.

Kant, I. 2009 (1793). Perpetual Peace. A Philosophical Sketch, in *An Answer to the Question: 'What is Enlightenment?'*. London: Penguin Books.

Leggewie, C. 2008. A Tour of the Battleground: The Seven Circles of Pan-European Memory. *Social Research*, 75:1, Spring.

Todorov, T. 2003. *Hope and Memory: Reflections on the Twentieth Century*. London: Atlantic Books.

Bibliography

Allen, A. 1996. Open Secret: a German Academic Hides His Past – in Plain Sight. *Lingua Franca*, April 1996, 28-41.
Adorno, T. 1967. Valéry Proust Museum, in *Prisms*, trans. Samuel and Shierry Webber. Cambridge, MA: MIT Press.
Adorno, T. 1986. What Does Coming to Terms with the Past Mean?, trans. Geoffrey Hartman, in *Bitburg in Moral and Political Perspective*. Indianapolis, IN: Indiana University Press, 114-129.
Alexander, J. 2002. On the Social Construction of Moral Universals. *European Journal of Social Theory*, 5:1, 5-85.
Alexander, J. et al. 2004. *Cultural Trauma and Collective Identity*. Berkeley, CA: University of California Press.
Anderson, B. 1991 (1983). *Imagined Communities: Reflections on the Origin and Spread of Nationalism*. London: Verso.
Appelbaum, A. 2003. *Gulag: A History*. New York: Penguin Books.
Arendt, H. 1958. *The Human Condition*. Chicago, IL: University of Chicago Press.
Arendt, H. 1963. *On Revolution*. New York: Penguin Books.
Arendt, H. 1963. *Eichmann in Jerusalem: A Report on the Banality of Evil*. New York: Penguin Books.
Arendt, H. 1968. Introduction. Walter Benjamin 1892-1940, in *Illuminations* by Walter Benjamin, New York: Schocken Books, 1-55.
Arendt, H. 1969. *Crises of the Republic*. New York: Harcourt Brace Jovanovich, 103-198.
Arendt, H. 1973 (1951). *The Origins of Totalitarianism*. New York: Harcourt Brace Jovanovich.
Arendt, H. 1978. *The Life of the Mind*. New York: Harcourt Brace Jovanovich.
Arendt, H. 1982. *Lectures on Kant's Political Philosophy*. Chicago, IL: University of Chicago Press.
Arendt, H. 1993 (1954). *Between Past and Future*. New York: Viking Press.
Arendt, H. 1994. *Essays in Understanding, 1930-1954*. New York: Harcourt Brace & Company.
Arendt, H. 2003. *Responsibility and Judgment*, edited by J. Kohn. New York: Schocken Books.
Arendt, H. 2005. *The Promise of Politics*, edited by J. Kohn. New York: Schocken Books.
Ash, T.G. 2001/2002. Mesomnesie: Pläydoyer für ein mittleres Erinnern. *Transit*, Winter, 32-48.

Ash, T.G. 2002. Trials, Purges and History Lessons: Treating a Difficult Past in Post-Communist Europe in *Memory and Power in Post-War Europe*, edited by Jan-Werner Müller. Cambridge: Cambridge University Press, 265-282.

Assmann, J. 1995. Collective Memory and Cultural Identity, trans. John Czaplicka. *New German Critique*, no. 65, Spring/Summer, 125-134.

Assmann, A. 2006. *Der lange Schatten der Vergangenheit: Erinnerungskultur und Geschichtspolitik.* Munich: C.H. Beck.

Astrov. A. 2008. Monumental Crisis: 'Nazis,' 'Occupiers' and Other Nihilists, in *Monumentaalne konflikt: Mälu, poliitika ja identiteet tänapäeva Eestis*. Tallinn: Varrak, 92-111.

Auer, S. 2006. The Lost Treasure of the Revolution. Originally published in *Osteuropa*, 9. Available at www.eurozine.com. Accessed November 19, 2010.

Barnouw, D. 1996. *Germany 1945: Views of War and Violence*. Bloomington, IN: Indiana University Press.

Barnouw, D. 2005. *The War in the Empty Air: Victims, Perpetrators, and Postwar Germans*. Bloomington, IN: Indiana University Press.

Barthes, R. 1972 (1957). *Mythologies*, trans. Annette Lavers, New York: Hill and Wang.

Bartov, O. 1996. *Murder in Our Midst: The Holocaust, Industrial Killing and Representation.* New York: Oxford University Press.

Baudrillard, J. 1983. *Simulations*, trans. Paul Foss, Paul Patton and Philip-Beitchman. New York: Semiotext(e).

Bauman, Z. 1989. *Modernity and the Holocaust*. Ithaca, NY: Cornell University Press.

Bauman, Z. 2000. *Liquid Modernity*. Cambridge: Polity Press.

Bauman, Z. 2008. *Does Ethics have a Chance in a World of Consumers?* Boston, MA: Harvard University Press.

Beevor, A. 2002. *Berlin: The Downfall 1945*. London: Penguin Books.

Bell, D. ed. 2006. *Memory, Trauma and World Politics: Reflections on the Relations between Past and Present.* London: Palgrave Macmillan.

Benjamin, W. 1968. Theses on the Philosophy of History, in *Illuminations*, trans. Harry Zohn. New York: Schocken Books, 253-267.

Benjamin, W. 1968. Unpacking my Library: A Talk about Book Collecting, in *Illuminations*. New York: Schocken Books.

Benjamin, W. 1968. Theses on the Philosophy of History, in *Illuminations*. New York: Schocken Books, 253-267.

Benhabib, S. 1990. Hannah Arendt and the Redemptive Power of Narrative. *Social Research*, 57:1, Spring, 167-196.

Benhabib, S. 2000. *The Reluctant Modernism of Hannah Arendt*. Lanham, MD: Rowman & Littlefield Publishers.

Berlin, I. 1998. My Intellectual Path in *The Power of Ideas*. Princeton, NJ: Princeton University Press, 1-23.

Berlin, I. 2003. The Pursuit of the Ideal, in *The Crooked Timber of Humanity: Chapters in the History of Ideas*. London: Pimlico, 1-19.

Bescançon, A. 2001. *Sajandi Õnnetus: Kommunismist, Natsismist ja Holokausti Ainulaadsusest*, trans. Katre Talviste. Tallinn: Loomingu Raamutukogu.
Bogorov, V. 2002. In the Temple of Sacred Motherland: Representations of National Identity in the Soviet and Russian WWII Memorials. Available at http://www.dartmouth.edu/~crn/groups/geographiers_group_papers/Finalpapers/Bogorov02.pdf. Accessed September 20, 2008.
Brüggemann, K. and Kasekamp, A. 2008. The Politics of Memory and the 'War of Monuments' in Estonia. *Nationalities Papers*, 36:3, July, 425-448.
Bude, H. 1992. *Bilanz der Nachfolge*. Frankfurt am Main: Suhrkamp.
Burke, P. 2004. *What is Cultural History?* Cambridge: Polity Press.
Challand, B. 2009 (1989), Contested Memories and the Shifting Cognitive Maps of Europe. *European Journal of Social Theory*, 12:3, August, 397-408.
Churchill, W. 1946. Speech given 19 September 1946 at Zurich University. Available at http://www.jef.at/cms/wp-content/uploads/churchill.pdf. Accessed November 10, 2009.
Confino, A. 2006. Collective Memory and Cultural History: Problems of Method in *Germany as a Culture of Remembrance: Promises and Limits of Writing History*. Chapel Hill: University of North Carolina Press.
Connerton, P. 1989. *How Societies Remember*. New York: Cambridge University Press.
Connerton, P. 2008. Seven Types of Forgetting. *Memory Studies*, 1:1, 59-71.
Cooper, B., ed. 1999. *War Crimes: The Legacy of Nuremberg*. New York: TV Books.
Dahrendorf, R. 1990. *Reflections on the Revolution in Europe*. New York: Times Books.
Davies, N. 2006. *Europe at War: 1939-1945. No Simple Victory*. London: Pan Books.
de Valk, E. 2010. The Pearl Divers. Hannah Arendt, Walter Benjamin and the Demands of History. *Krise: Journal for Contemporary Philosophy*, Issue 1. Available at http://www.krisis.eu/content/2010-1/krisis-2010-1-04-devalk.pdf. Accessed November 12, 2010.
Diner, D. ed. 1987. *Ist der Nationalsozialismus Geschichte? Zu Historisierung und Historikerstreit*. Frankfurt am Main: Fischer.
Diner, D. 2003. Restitution and Memory: The Holocaust in European Political Cultures. *New German Critique*. Fall, 90, 36-44.
Dubiel, H. 2003. The Remembrance of the Holocaust as a Catalyst for a Transnational Ethic? *New German Critique*, Fall, 90, 59-70.
Endlich, S. and Lutz, T. 1995. *Gedenken und Lernen an Historischen Orten: Ein Wegweiser zu Gedenkstätten für die Opfer des Nationalsozialismus in Berlin*. Berlin: Landeszentrale für politische Bildungsarbeit.
EPP-ED. Group in the European Parliament. Resolution adopted by the XVIth EEP Congress Condemning totalitarian Communism. February 4-5, 2004. http://www.epp-ed.eu/Press/peve04/eve01/res-communism_en.asp? Accessed April 26, 2008.

Erelt, P. 2007. Kui monumente teisaldati dünamiidiga (When Monuments are Relocated with Dynamite). *Eesti Ekspress*, January 30. www.ekspress.ee/print /266851090B9FC7C2257273003A71EA. Accessed March 15, 2007.
Estonia 1940-1945. Available at www.historycommission.ee.
European Parliament Resolution on European Conscience and Totalitarianism. 2009. Available at http://www.europarl.europa.eu/pdfs/news/expert/infopress /20090401IPR53245/20090401IPR53245_en.pdf. Accessed April 3, 2009.
Finkielkraut, A. 1995. *The Defeat of the Mind*, trans. Judith Friedlander. New York: Columbia University Press.
Forever in the Shadow of Hitler? The Dispute about the German Understanding of History. 1993, trans. James Knowlton and Truett Cates. Highlands: Humanities Press.
Foundation. 2008. Foundation for the Investigation of the Communist Crimes. Estonia to Probe Soviet-era Abuses. February 1, 2008. Available at http://www.haaba.com/news/2008/02/01/7-84989/estonia-to-probe-sovietera-abuses.html. Accessed January 28, 2009.
Freud, S. 2003. *The Uncanny*, trans. David McLintock. New York: Penguin Books.
Friedlander, S. ed. 1992. *Probing the Limits of Representation: Nazism and the "Final Solution'*. Cambridge, MA: Harvard University Press.
Gadamer, H.G. 1975. *Truth and Method*, trans. Joel Winsheimer and Donald G. Marshall. New York: Crosswood Publishing.
Gadamer, H.G. 1989. Die Vielfalt Europas Erbe und Zukunft, in *Das Erbe Europas*. Frankfurt: Suhrkamp, 7-34.
Gibson, W. 1999. 'My Obsession'. *Wired*, April 7. Available at www.wired.com/wired/archive/7.01<7ebay.html. Accessed April 8, 2010.
Giesen, B. 2004. *Triumph and Trauma*. Boulder, CO: Paradigm Publishers.
Gleick, J. 1998. Fast Forward, the Digital Attic: an Archive of Everything. *The New York Times*, April 12. Available at http://www.nytimes.com/1998/04/12/magazine/fast-forward-the-digital-attic-an-archive-of-everything.html?n=Top/Reference/Times%20Topics/People/G/Gleick,%20James&pagewanted=all. Accessed April 8, 2010.
Gleick, J. 1999. *Faster: The Acceleration of Just about Everything*. New York: Pantheon Books.
Goldhagen, D. 1996. *Hitler's Willing Executioners: Ordinary Germans and the Holocaust*. New York: Knopf Press.
Grass, G. 2003/2004. *Crabwalk*. New York: Harvest Books.
Grass, G. 2006/2007. *Peeling the Onion*. New York: Harvest Books.
Grunenberg, A. 1993. *Antifaschismus: Ein deutscher Mythos*. Hamburg: Rowohlt.
Gudkov, L. 2005. The Fetters of Victory. How the War provides Russia with its Identity. *Osteuropa*, 4-6. Accessed in *Eurozine*, March 13, 2007. www.eurozine.xom/articles/2005-05-03-gudkov-en.html, 5.
Habermas, J. 1993. On the Public Use of History: The Official Self-Understanding of the Federal Republic is Breaking Up in *Forever in the Shadow of Hitler?*, trans. James Knowlton and Truett Cates. Highlands, NJ: Humanities Press.

Habermas, J. 2001. The Postnational Constellation and the Future of Democracy, in *The Postnational Constellation: Political Essays*. London: Polity Press, 58-112.

Hackmann, J. 2009. From National Victims to Transnational Bystanders? The Changing Commemoration of World War II in Central and Eastern Europe. *Constellations: An International Journal of Critical and Democratic Theory*, 16:1, March, 167-181.

Halbwachs, M. 1980 (1950). *The Collective Memory*, trans. Francis J. Ditter, Jr. and Vida Yazdi Ditter. New York: Harper Colophon.

Halbwachs, M. 1992 (1941). *On Collective Memory*, trans. Lewis A. Coser. Chicago, IL: University of Chicago Press.

Herder, J.G. 1993. *Against Pure Reason: Writings on Religion, Language and History*, trans. Marcia Bunge, Minneapolis, MN: Ausburg Fortress Press.

Hiio, T. et al., 2006. *Estonia 1940-1945: Reports of the Estonian International Commission for the Investigation of Crimes against Humanity.* Tallinn: Estonian Foundation for the Investigation of Crimes against Humanity.

Historikerstreit: Die Dokumentation der Kontroverse um die Einzigartigkeit der nationalsozialistischen Judenvernichtung, 1987. Munich: Piper.

Hobsbawm, E. 1983. Mass-Producing Traditions: Europe, 1870-1914, in *The Invention of Tradition*, edited by Eric Hobsbawm and Terence Ranger. Cambridge: Cambridge University Press, 263-307.

Holocaust Forum. 2000. Stockholm, January 2000. Available at www.holocaustforum.gov.se.

Huyssen, A. 1995. *Twilight Memories: Marking Time in a Culture of Amnesia*. New York: Routledge Publishing.

Huyssen, A. 2003. *Present Pasts: Urban Palimpsests and the Politics of Memory*. Palo Alto, CA: Stanford University Press.

Inglis, K. 1993.Grabmäler für Unbekannte Soldaten, in *Die Neue Wache unter den Linden: Ein Deutsches Denkmal im Wandel der Geschichte*. Berlin: Koehler & Amelang, 150-171.

Ilves, T.H. 2007 Eesti ei kirjuta oma ajalugu ümber. *Eesti Päevaleht*, February 3.

Ilves, T.H. 2008. Speech at the presidential conference. Erinevad mälud – ühine ulevik [Different memories – common future]. November 21, 2008. Available at: http://www.president.ee/print.me.php?gid=122202. Accessed December 12, 2008.

Jaspers, K. 1961 (1947). *The Question of German Guilt*, trans. E.B. Ashton. New York: Capricorn Books.

Jaspers, K. 2000. *Karl Jaspers: Basic Philosophical Writings*, trans. and edited by Edith Ehrlich et al. Amherst, NY: Humanity Books.

Judt, T. 2002. The Past is Another Country: Myth and Memory in Post-war Europe, in *Memory and Power in Post-War Europe*, edited by Jan-Werner Müller, London: Cambridge University Press, 157-183.

Judt, T. 2005. *Postwar: A History of Europe since 1945.* New York: Penguin Press.

Judt, T. 2008. *Reappraisals: Reflections on the Forgotten Twentieth Century*. New York: Penguin Books.
Kaasik, P. 2006. Tõnismäe pronkssõdur. *Akadeemia*, 18:9, 1891-1918.
Kalyvas, A. 2008. *Democracy and the Politics of the Extraordinary: Max Weber, Carl Schmitt and Hannah Arendt*. Cambridge: Cambridge University Press.
Kant, I. 1981 (1785). *Grounding for the Metaphysics of Morals*, trans. James W. Ellington. Indianapolis, IN: Hackett Publishing Company.
Kant, I. 2009 (1793). Perpetual Peace. A Philosophical Sketch, in *An Answer to the Question: 'What is Enlightenment?'*. London: Penguin Books.
Kateb, G. 2000. Political Action: Its Nature and Advantages, in *The Cambridge Companion to Hannah Arendt*, edited by Dana Villa. Cambridge: Cambridge University Press, 130-148.
Kattago, S. 1998. Representing German Victimhood and Guilt: The Neue Wache and Unified German Memory. *German Politics and Society*, 16:3, 86-104.
Kõresaar, E. 2005. *Elu Ideoloogiad: Kollektiivne mälu ja autobiograafiline minevikutõlgendus eestlaste elulugedes (Ideologies of Life: Collective Memory and Autobiographical Meaning-Making of the Past in Estonian Life Stories)*. Tartu: Eesti Rahva Muuseum.
Koselleck, R. 1985. *Futures Past: On the Semantics of Historical Time*, trans. Keith Tribe. Cambridge, MA: MIT Press.
Koselleck, R. 1993. Bilderverbot, in *Die Neue Wache unter den Linden: Ein deutsches Denkmal im Wandel der Geschichte*, edited by Christoph Stölzl. Berlin: Koehler & Amelang, 200-203.
Koselleck, R. and Jeismann, M., eds. 1994. *Der politische Totenkult: Kriegerdenkmäler in der Moderne*. Munich: Wilhelm Fink Verlag.
Koselleck, R. 2001/2002. Die Transformation der Politischen Totenmale im 20. Jahrhundert. *Transit: Ein europäisches Revue*, 22, Winter 2001/2002, 59-86.
Koselleck, R. 2002. *The Practice of Conceptual History: Timing History, Spacing Concepts*, trans. Todd Samuel Pressner, Palo Alto, CA: Stanford University Press.
Koselleck, R. 2004. Gibt es ein kollektives Gedächtnis? *Divinatio*, 19:2 (Spring), 1-6.
Kracauer, S. 1995. The Mass Ornament, in *The Mass Ornament: Weimar Essays*, trans. Thomas Y. Levin. Cambridge, MA: Harvard University Press.
Lagerspetz, M. 1999. Postsocialism as a Return: Notes on a Discursive Strategy. *East European Politics and Societies*, 13:2, 377-390.
Lebow, R.N. 2006. The Memory of Politics in Postwar Europe, in *The Politics of Memory in Postwar Europe*, edited by Richard Ned Lebow, Wulf Kansteiner, Claudio Fogu. Durham, NC: Duke University Press, 1-39.
Leggewie, C. 1995. Ein irritierendes Lehrstück. *DUZ: Das Hochschulmagazin*, July 7, 1995, 14-16.
Leggewie, C. 1998. *Von Schneider zu Schwerte: Das ungewöhliche Leben eines Mannes, der aus der Geschichte lernen wollte*. Vienna: Carl Hanser Verlag.

Leggewie, C. 2006. Equally Criminal? Totalitarian Experience and European Memory. Originally in *Transit*, June 2006. Available www.eurozine.com Accessed August 18, 2008.

Leggewie, C. 2008. A Tour of the Battleground: The Seven Circles of Pan-European Memory. *Social Research*, 75:1, Spring.

Lin, M. 2006. Available at www.vvmf.org/POPUP_printing.cfm?sectionID=77, October 23.

Lowenthal, D. 1985. *The Past is a Foreign Country*. New York: Cambridge University Press.

Lübbe, H. 1983. Der Nationalsozialismus im politischen Bewusstein der Gegenwart, in *Deutschlands Weg in die Diktatur: Internationale Konferenz zur nationalsoizialistischen Machtübername in Reichstagsgebäude zu Berlin. Referate und Diskussion. Ein Protokoll*. Berlin, 329-349.

Lübbe, H. 1983. *Zeit-Verhältnisse: Zur Kulturphilosophie des Fortschritts*. Graz/Vienna/Cologne: Verlag Styria.

Lübbe, H. 1992. *Im Zug der Zeit: Verkürzter Aufenthalt in der Gegenwart*. Berlin: Springer Verlag.

Lübbe, H. 2007. *Von Parteigenossen zum Bundesbürger: Über beschwiegene und historische Vergangenheiten*. Wilhelm Fink.

Lübbe, H. 2009. The Contraction of the Present, in *High-Speed Society: Social Acceleration, Power and Modernity*, edited by Hartmut Rosa and William E. Scheuerman. University Park, PA: Pennsylvania State Press, 159-178.

Maier, C.S. 1988. *The Unmasterable Past: History, Holocaust and German National Identity*. Cambridge, MA: Harvard University Press.

Maier, C.S. 2002. Hot Memory ... Cold Memory: On the Political Half-Life of Fascist and Communist Memory. *Transit: Europäische Revue*, Number 22, Winter 2001/2002, 153-165. Available at http://www.iwm.at/index2.php?option=com_content&task=view&id=316&Itemid=481. Accessed February 24, 2008.

Mannheim, K. 1928/1952. The Problem of Generations. *Essays on the Sociology of Knowledge*. London: Routledge and Kegan Paul. 276-322.

Marchart, O. 2006. Time for a New Beginning. Arendt, Benjamin, and the Messanic Conception of Political Temporality. *Redescriptions: Yearbook of Political Thought and Conceptual History*, 134-147.

Margalit, A. 2002. *The Ethics of Memory*. Cambridge, MA: Harvard University Press.

Marx, K. 1978 (1852). *The Eighteenth Brumaire of Louis Bonaparte*, Peking: Foreign Languages Press.

Mayr, W. 1995. Ich bin doch immun. *Der Spiegel*, 19/1995, 94-97.

'MEPs call for EU stance on Communist Crimes.' 2008. http://euobservor.com/9/26021?rss_rk=1 April 22. Accessed April 26, 2008.

Minow, M. 1998. *Between Vengeance and Forgiveness: Facing History after Genocide and Mass Violence*. Boston: Beacon Press.

Mitscherlich, A. and M. 1975. *The Inability to Mourn*, trans. Veberly R. Placzek. New York: Grove Press.

Misztal, B.A. 2004. The Sacralization of Memory. *European Journal of Social Theory*, 7:1, 67-84.
Misztal, B.A. 2005. Memory and Democracy. *American Behavioral Scientist*, 48:10, June, 1320-38.
Mosse, G.L. 1990. *Fallen Soldiers: Reshaping the Memory of World Wars.* Oxford: Oxford University Press.
Motyl, A.J. 2008. Warum ist die KGB-Bar möglich? *Transit*, 35, Summer, 104-122.
Mouffe, C. 2000. *The Democratic Paradox.* London: Verso.
Mouffe, C. 2002. Politics and Passions: The Stakes of Democracy. *CSC Perspectives Working Papers*. Available at http://www.wmin.ac.uk/sshl/page-221. Accessed April 22, 2009.
Mouffe, C. 2005 (1992). *The Return of the Political*. London: Verso.
Mouffe C. 2007. Artistic Activism and Agonistic Politics. *Art and Research: A Journal of Ideas, Contexts and Methods*, 1:2, Summer, 1-5.
Müller, J.-W. ed. *Memory and Power in Post-War Europe.* Cambridge: Cambridge University Press, 157-183.
Musil, R. 1995. Monuments, in *Posthumous Papers of a Living Author*, trans. Peter Wortsman. New York: Penguin, 61-64.
Nietzsche, F. 1980 (1874). *On the Advantage and Disadvantage of History for Life*, trans. Peter Preuss. Indianapolis, IN: Hackett Publishing.
Nora, P. 1989. Between Memory and History: Les Lieux de Mémoire. *Representations*, 26, Spring: 7-25.
Nora, P. 1996. General Introduction: Between Memory and History, in *Realms of Memory: The Construction of the French Past*, edited by Pierre Nora. New York: Columbia University Press.
Nora, P. 2002. Reasons for the Current Upsurge in Memory. *Eurozine*. Available at http://www.eurozine.com/articles/2002-04-19-nora-en.html. Accessed March 13, 2007.
Oathwaite, W. and Ray, L. 2005. Modernity, Memory and Postcommunism, in S*ocial Theory and Postcommunism.* London: Blackwell, 176-196.
Olick, J.K. 2003. The Value of Regret? Lessons from and for Germany, in *Justice and the Politics of Memory: Religion and Public Life*, edited by Gabriel. R. Ricci. New Brunswick, NJ: Transaction Books, 21-32.
Olick, J.K. 2005. *In the House of the Hangman: The Agonies of German Defeat. 1943-1949.* Chicago, IL: University of Chicago Press.
Olick. J.K. 2007. From Usable Pasts to the Return of the Repressed. *Hedgehog Review*, 9:2.
Olick, J.K. 2007. *The Politics of Regret: On Collective Memory and Historical Responsibility*. New York: Routledge.
Olschowsky, B. 2008. Erinnerungslandschaft mit Brücken. *Transit*, 35, Summer, 23-49.

Onken, E.C. 2007. The Baltic States and Moscow's 9 May Commemoration: Analysing Memory Politics in Europe. *Europe-Asia Studies*, 59:1, January, 23-46.

Onken, E.C. 2007. The Politics of Finding Historical Truth: Reviewing Baltic History Commissions and their Work. *Journal of Baltic Studies*, 38:1, 109-116.

Petersoo, P. and Tamm, M. eds. 2008. *Monumentaalne konflikt: Mälu, poliitika ja identiteet tänapäeva Eestis* (*Monumental Conflict: Memory, Politics and Identity in Contemporary Estonia*). Tallinn: Varrak.

Popper, K. 1966 (1945). *The Open Society and its Enemies*. Vols 1 and 2. London: Routledge.

Reichel, P. 1995. *Politik mit der Erinnerung: Gedächnisorte im Streit um die nationalsozialistische Vergangenheit*. Munich: Carl Hanser Verlag.

Renan, E. 1990. What is a Nation, in *Nation and Narration*. New York: Routledge, 8-22.

Ricoeur, P. 1991. The Human Experience of Time and Narrative, in *A Ricoeur Reader: Reflection and Imagination*. Toronto: University of Toronto Press.

Rorty, R. 1989. *Contingency, Irony and Solidarity*. Cambridge: Cambridge University Press.

Santayana, G. 1998. *The Life of Reason*. Amherst: Prometheus Books.

Schaap, A. 2007. Political Theory and the Agony of Politics. *Political Studies Review*, 5, 56-74.

Schlink, B. 1998. *The Reader*, trans. Carol Brown Janeway, New York: Vintage Books.

Schlink, B. 2009. *Guilt about the Past*. Toronto: Ananasi Press.

Schmitt, C. 1979 (1932). *The Concept of the Political*, trans. G Schwab. Chicago, IL: University of Chicago Press.

Schwan, G. 2001. *Politics and Guilt: The Destructive Power of Silence*, trans. Thomas Dunlap. Lincoln, NE: University of Nebraska Press.

Sebald, W.G. 1999/2004. *On the Natural History of Destruction*. New York: Modern Library.

Shakespeare, W. 1987. *The Tempest*. Oxford: Oxford University Press.

Shils, E. 1981. *Tradition*. Chicago, IL: University of Chicago Press.

Smith, A.D. 2003. *Chosen Peoples: Sacred Sources of National Identity*. Oxford: Oxford University Press.

Smith, D. 2002. Estonia: Indendence and European Integration, in M. Lehti and D.J. Smith, eds, *The Baltic States: Estonia, Latvia and Lithuania*. London: Routledge.

Snyder, T. 2005. Balancing the Books. *Index on Censorship*, Number 2. Available at www.eurozine.com. Accessed November 11, 2009.

Snyder, T. 2010. *Bloodlands: Europe Between Hitler and Stalin*. New York: Basic Books.

Sontag, S. 1990 (1973). *On Photography*. New York: Anchor Books.

Sontag, S. 2003. *Regarding the Pain of Others*. New York: Picador.

Stölzl, C. ed. 1993. *Die Neue Wache unter den Linden: Ein Deutsches Denkmal im Wandel der Geschichte.* Berlin: Koehler & Amelang.
The Economist. 2007. The Rewriting of History. November 8.
Todorov, T. 2003. *Hope and Memory: Reflections on the Twentieth Century.* London: Atlantic Books.
Vetik, R. 2006. Reactive Identity versus EU Integration. *JCMS*, 44:5, 1079-1102.
Vico, G. 1948. *The New Science of Giambattista Vico*, trans. T.G. Bergin and M.H Fisch. Ithaca, NY Cornell University Press.
Vihalemm, T. and Lauristin, M. 1997. Cultural Adjustment to the Changing Societal Environment: The Case of Russians in Estonia in *Return to the Western World*, Tartu: Tartu University Press, 279-297.
Von Weizsäcker, R. 1985. Speech by Richard von Weizsäcker, President of the Federal Republic of Germany, in the Bundestag during the Ceremony Commemorating the 40th Anniversary of the End of the War in Europe and of National Socialist Tyranny, May 8, 1985 in *Bitburg in Moral and Political Perspective*, edited by Geoffrey Hartman. Bloomington, IN: Indiana University Press, 263-273.
Wagner-Pacifici, R. and Schwartz, B. 1991. The Vietnam Veterans Memorial: Commemorating a Difficult Past. *American Journal of Sociology*, 97, September 1991, 376-420.
Wertsch, J. 2008. Collective Memory and Narrative Templates. *Social Research*, 75:1, Spring, 133-156.
Winter, J. 1995. *Sites of Memory, Sites of Mourning: The Great War in European Cultural History*. Cambridge: Cambridge University Press.
Wolf, C. 1975. *Patterns of Childhood*, trans. Ursule Molinaro, New York: Noonday Press.
Wulf, M. 2007. The struggle for official recognition of 'displaced' group memories in post-Soviet Estonia in *Past in the Making: Recent History Revisions and Historical Revisionism in Central Europe after 1989*, Michal Kopecek, eds. Budapest and New York: Central European Press, 217-241.
Young, J. 1993. *The Texture of Memory: Holocaust Memorials and Meaning*. New Haven and London: Yale University Press.
Zelizer, B. 1998. *Remembering to Forget: Holocaust Memory Through the Camera's Eye*. Chicago, IL: University of Chicago Press.
Zhurzhenko, T. 2007. The Geopolitics of Memory. *Transit*, 10 May, 2007. Available at www.eurozine.com. Accessed September 12, 2008.

Index

Adorno, Theodor 3, 6, 31, 109
Alexander, Jeffrey
   and trauma 30, 36
Antifascism, myth of 84-85
Appelbaum, Anne 23, 34, 38
Arendt, Hannah 13-14, 40-42, 63-65, 97-99, 101-104,106,125
   and the banality of evil 14, 71-73
   and revolution 109-120
Archiving and memory 8-11
Ash, Timothy Garton 12, 18-21, 24-25, 123-124
Assmann, Aleida 68
Assmann, Jan 35
Aufarbeitung der Vergangenheit 18, 31, *see also* coming to terms with the past and *Vergangenheitsbewältigung*
Auschwitz 32-33

Banality of evil, *see* Arendt, Hannah
Barnouw, Dagmar 13, 32, 50-56
Barthes, Roland
   and myth 84-85
Baudrillard, Jean 6
Bauman, Zygmunt 3-5, 7, 32, 123, 126
Benhabib, Seyla 99, 109-120
Benjamin, Walter 3, 9, 14, 118-120
Berlin, Isaiah 13-14, 39-41, 97, 102-105
Besançon, Alain 24
Bogorov, Valentin 85
Bronze Soldier monument, history of 20, 77-80, 84, 86-91
Bude, Hans 31-32, 61
Burke, Edmund 101, 109
Burke, Peter 30

Collecting and memory 9-10
Collective guilt, *see* guilt
Collective memory, *see* memory

Coming to terms with the past 12, 18, 25, 31, 68-69, *see* *Vergangenheitsbewältigung* also *Aufarbeitung der Vergangenheit*
Connerton, Paul 19, 29

Dahrendorf, Ralf 101-102
Davies, Norman 23, 34
Democratization of history 1, 21, 30-32, 50, 78, 93
Dubiel, Helmut 36

Eichmann, Adolf 36, 61, 63, 71-74
Empathy 27, 39-42, 81, 103-105,126
Ethics of memory, *see* Margalit, Avashi

Forgetting and memory, *see* memory
Freud, Sigmund 20, 30-31, 67, 69-71
Friedländer, Saul 32, 49-50

Gadamer, Hans-Georg 2, 14, 28-29, 32, 40, 126-127
Generations
   and guilt 61-66
   and Mannheim 34
   and memory 32, 35
Gleick, James 10-11
Goldhagen, David 63-64
Great Patriotic War 33, 35, 77, 84-85, 87-88, 92, 100
Guilt and silence 59-66,
   collective guilt 22-23, 51-53, 56, 62, 64-65, 97, 99-101, 106, *see also* generations
Gudkov, Lev 33, 88-89

Habermas, Jürgen 33, 98, 102, 104
Halbwachs, Maurice 14-15, 21-23, 29-30, 54, 90
Herder, Johann Gottfried 39, 103

Historians' debate, West German 36-37
History, democratization of, *see* democratization of history
Hobsbawm, Eric 30, 80, 124
Holocaust
   and modernity 3, 34
   and trauma 30-32,
   and World War II 12, 23-24, 27, 30-39, 42-43
Holocaust Forum 35-36
Huyssen, Andreas 3, 5-6

Ilves, Toomas Hendrik 38, 105-106

Jaspers, Karl 19, 53, 62
Judgment 9, 28, 53, 59, 61, 65-66, 72, 125, *see also* phronesis
Judt, Tony 12, 14, 23, 34, 36-37, 84, 92, 99-100, 124-125

Kant, Immanuel 39, 41, 72, 103, 125-127
Kolokowski, Leszek 61-62
Kõresaar, Ene 34, 90-91
Koselleck, Reinhart
   on time 1-4, 7, 21-23, 29,
   on war memorials 78-82, 93
Kracauer, Siegfried 9

Leggewie, Claus
   comparing Nazism and communism 37
   on Schneider/Schwerte 68, 71, 73-74, 123-124
Lieux de mémoire, *see* Nora, Pierre
Lübbe, Hans
   on time 6-7,
   on silence and democracy 19, 62-63, 69, 74

Maier, Charles 37-38
Mannheim
   and generations 34
Margalit, Avashai
   and ethics of memory 36, 100
Marx, Karl 4, 77
Mass media and memory, *see* memory

Memory
   collective 21-23, 25, 27, 29-30, 49, 56, 59, 90
   and forgetting 7-8, 14, 18-19, 24-25, 55, 59, 69, 90
   and mass media 1, 5-10, 32
   and time 1-4, *see also* archiving, collecting, generations, responsibility
Minow, Martha 31, 36, 61
Misztal, Barbara 19, 24, 100
Mnemosyne 12, 29
Modernity 1-5,7, 12-13, 15-16, 21-23, 32, 35, 113,123-125
   liquid modernity 4-5
   and mass media 5-9
Molotov-Ribbentrop Pact 33, 37
Mosse, George 78, 80-81
Mouffe, Chantal 13, 98-99, 102-103, 106
Musil, Robert 77

Narratives of World War II 12-13, 23, 27-28, 32-36, 42, 92, 97, 99
Nazism and communism, comparing 35-39
Neue Wache memorial 83-84, 86
Nietzsche, Friedrich 6-9, 11, 17-18, 24, 30, 59, 124
Nora, Pierre 1-4, 10, 14, 21, 29-30

Olick, Jeffrey 30-32, 36, 61
Onken, Eva-Clarita 27, 38, 88
Open society 17-18, 25,
   and Popper 101-104

Phronesis 125, *see* judgment, Arendt, Hannah
Pluralism 14, 18, 27, 31, 97
   and empathy 39-43
   and open society 99-106
Popper, Karl 101-104

Renan, Ernst 19
Resolution on European Conscience and Totalitarianism 37-38

Responsibility and memory 13, 19-20, 23, 25, 31, 62-65, 84, 89, 101, 105-106

Santayana, George 104
Schaap, Andrew 103
Schlink, Bernhard 13, 59-61, 64-66
Schmitt, Carl 13, 97-99, 103, 106
Schneider/Schwerte, Hans 13, 76-74
Schwan, Gesine 13, 19-20, 31-32, 59-66
Screen memories 69-70, *see also* Freud, Sigmund
Sebald, W.G. 32, 53
Smith, Anthony 79
Smith, David 91
Snyder, Timothy 23-24, 34
Sontag, Susan 13-14, 21-23, 37, 49-51, 54-56
Soviet war memorials 84-86

Time 1-7, 11-14, 19-21, 24, 39, 56, 89-93
    revolutionary time 117-120, *see also* Lübbe, Hans
Todorov, Tzvetan 23-24, 123

Trauma 28-35, 65, 77, 81-84, 88-91, 104, 123

Uncanny 6, 12-13, 67, 69-75, *see also* Freud, Sigmund
Unknown Soldier memorials 78-81, 86-87

War memorials
    and Koselleck, *see* Koselleck
Vergangenheitsbewältigung 18, 31
    see also coming to terms with the past and *Aufarbeitung der Vergangenheit*
Vico, Giambattista 39-40, 102-103
Vietnam Veterans' Memorial 82-84

Winter, Jay 80
Wolf, Christa 68-69, 74

Young, James
    and Holocaust memory 50, 81

Zelizer, Barbie 13, 50-51, 53-56

For Product Safety Concerns and Information please contact our EU
representative GPSR@taylorandfrancis.com
Taylor & Francis Verlag GmbH, Kaufingerstraße 24, 80331 München, Germany

www.ingramcontent.com/pod-product-compliance
Lightning Source LLC
Chambersburg PA
CBHW061843300426
44115CB00013B/2486